# PERFECT PHRASES in

## Spanish

## for Confident Travel
## to Mexico

### The No *Faux-Pas* Phrasebook
### for the Perfect Trip

Eric Vogt

New York  Chicago  San Francisco  Lisbon  London  Madrid  Mexico City
Milan  New Delhi  San Juan  Seoul  Singapore  Sydney  Toronto

The McGraw·Hill Companies

**Library of Congress Cataloging-in-Publication Data**

Vogt, Eric W.
　　　Perfect phrases in Spanish for confident travel to Mexico / by Eric
W. Vogt.
　　　　　　p.　　cm. — (Perfect phrases for the perfect trip)
　　　English and Spanish
　　　ISBN 0-07-160481-2 (alk. paper)
　　　1. Spanish language—Textbooks for foreign speakers—
English.　　2. Mexico—Description and travel.　　[I. Spanish language—
Conversation and phrase books—English.]　　I. Title.

　PC4121.V66　　2009
　468.3'421—dc22　　　　　　　　　　　　　　2008051248

1 2 3 4 5 6 7 8 9 10 11 12 13 14 15 16 17 18 19 20 FGR/FGR　0 9

ISBN　978-0-07-160481-9
MHID　　0-07-160481-2

McGraw-Hill books are available at special quantity discounts to use as
premiums and sales promotions or for use in corporate training programs.
To contact a representative, please visit the Contact Us pages at
www.mhprofessional.com.

This book is printed on acid-free paper.

# Contents

Acknowledgments     v
Introduction     vii
Pronunciation Guide     xi

Chapter 1     Good Manners                          1

Chapter 2     Money                                 9

Chapter 3     Public Transportation                17

Chapter 4     Shopping                             27

Chapter 5     Shopping for Food                    35

Chapter 6     Friendship and Romance               43

Chapter 7     Hotels                               53

Chapter 8     Eating Out                           63

Chapter 9     Entertainment                        73

Chapter 10    Museums                              83

Chapter 11    Common Warning Signs                 93

Chapter 12    Health Issues                       101

Chapter 13    Emergencies                         111

# Contents

Chapter 14   Making Plans                                    119

Chapter 15   Keeping in Touch                                131

Chapter 16   Weather                                         141

Chapter 17   Sports and Gambling                             151

Chapter 18   Pyramids and Ruins                              163

Chapter 19   Seaside: Diving, Sunbathing,
             and Surfing                                     173

Chapter 20   Conversational Phrases                          183

# Acknowledgments

Thanks are very much in order to my administrative assistant, Ms. Marilyn Hancock, who knows no Spanish and was so willing to read aloud the phrases using the pronunciation guide.

My most heartfelt thanks go to my dear wife, Arlene, and my sweet daughter, Alexandra, neither of whom ever doubted that I would succeed in taking on a quick succession of these projects. Words can never express the comfort and energy their confidence in me has supplied. To them and, of course, to all who travel for business or pleasure, I dedicate this little volume.

Finally, I give my hearfelt thanks to my editor at McGraw-Hill Garret Lemoi for is patience and encouragement throughout this project. Without his skillful guidance, I never would have finished this phrasebook.

# Introduction

*Travel to Mexico.* The phrase evokes as many images as there are ears to hear it. There are many Mexicos. As a nation, Mexico is a mosaic of old and new, of native peoples, Europeans, and, of course, of the mostly *mestizo* population that resulted from what the Mexicans refer to not as the Discovery of America, but as the Encounter of Two Worlds with the Conquest of Mexico by Hernán Cortés in 1521.

One of Mexico's great intellectuals of modern times, Octavio Paz, observed that a pyramid is a good image through which to understand Mexico's diversity. He noted that there are Mexicans who live almost untouched by the arrival of the Europeans, though they are fewer and fewer every day. There are others who live in an almost medieval European world, and then there are those who live much like anyone in a wealthy borough of New York City or San Francisco.

Mexicans tend to be very hospitable and friendly. I'm sure you've heard the expression *Mi casa es su casa* (My house is your house). When a Mexican says this, it is not a casual statement. It is genuine. Likewise, if an American says it to a Mexican, it will be taken as a serious invitation to make himself or herself at home in your place, without necessarily announcing their arrival. Inviting someone to lunch is taken seriously, unlike the often meaningless "let's do lunch" one hears in the United States.

That said, Mexicans tend to observe formalities in forms of address and are sensitive about etiquette and good manners. The best way to grasp this is to remember that being on a first-name basis with Mexicans is not something that happens as quickly as it does in the United States. When it comes to initiating a change in the level of formality, it is best to allow them to take the lead, because they will initiate the change according to the rules of their culture.

Racially and socioeconomically, Mexico is quite diverse. In terms of her geography and climate, she can be divided roughly into three east-west bands from north to south. In the north, she shares the desert climate of the four U.S. states that border her six. This is her industrial region, though agriculture is also a major source of revenue. In the middle she is semi-arid, more seasonal, and densely populated. This is where Mexico City is located. It is where most of her great universities and hubs of political power are located. Lastly, the south is tropical, economically poor, and culturally rich. The south of Mexico is where the bulk of her pure native populations is found and where many people do not speak Spanish. This is where one may visit the Mayan ruins and the jungles of Yucatán. On the coasts of Yucatán one finds Cancún, Cozumel, and other favorite tourist destinations, famous for their five-star hotels, beaches, food, reef diving, and so forth. Mexico's west coast is probably best known by Americans because it is so accessible from California and Arizona, whether by car, bus, train, plane, or boat. The west coast includes Baja California (divided politically into Norte and Sur), La Paz, Puerto Peñasco (with its English name, *Rocky Point*), Guaymas, Mazatlán, Puerto Vallarta, Ixtapa, and Acapulco, to mention the major cities where many people from north of the border go for sun, relaxation, and deep-sea fishing.

As culturally rich and inviting as Mexico is, this phrasebook is for the traveler with little or no knowledge of Spanish. It offers tourists and business travelers what they need to make their short visits more comfortable in terms of the amenities they likely already enjoy at home in the United States or Canada. No knowledge of grammar is necessary to make use of this phrasebook immediately.

The pronunciation guide for this phrasebook has been designed to be as intuitive as possible for English speakers. With only a few minutes of practice, readers should be able to be understood by anyone who hears them.

The phrases included in this book will help you communicate with Spanish speakers throughout your trip to Mexico, from such basic courtesy-related phrases as *Buenas tardes, señora,* which are useful in setting the tone for any situation, and more situation-specific phrases designed to help you out with essential needs such as checking into a hotel or ordering in a restaurant. The organization of phrases within the book is based on major themes such as hotels, money, shopping, and entertainment. There are also some conversational phrases for those who would like to forge relationships with Spanish speakers.

Each chapter includes several main entries covering a specific situation or need, such as *Tengo una reservación para dos* (I have a reservation for two). Each entry is accompanied by detailed explanations of the cultural context in which you might encounter or use these phrases, enabling you to make the most of your encounters with Spanish speakers during your trip. Each main entry is also followed by other phrases that reinforce or pertain to the main entry that will greatly increase your ability to communicate.

Finally, one bit of advice from another famous Mexican writer, diplomat, and intellectual Carlos Fuentes bears paraphrasing because it is too often forgotten by some visitors. Mexico is a sovereign country with her own history and laws. She has her own rules, her own language and customs, even though she invites and warmly welcomes all to enjoy her resorts and many amusements.

# Pronunciation Guide

For practical purposes Spanish has only five vowel sounds, as opposed to English, which has approximately fourteen "shades" of the same five vowels of the alphabet: *a, e, i, o,* and *u.* Each of them has one sound only, in all contexts. They are pronounced as follows; the manner in which their pronunciation will be shown in this guide is given in parentheses:

- **a** (ah) is pronounced as in the English word *father,* never as in *hat* or as in *awe*
- **e** (eh) is pronounced as in the English words *way* or *say,* never as in *met,* but without continuing into the sound represented by the letter *y* in these English words
- **i** (ee) is pronounced as in the English word *meet,* never as in *sit*
- **o** (o) is pronounced as in the English word *over,* never as in *not*
- **u** (oo) is pronounced as in the English words *cool* or *soon,* never as in *mud*

Whenever two vowels come together, even when one is at the end of one word and the other at the beginning of another, they elide, or form a single syllable. A syllable is defined as an utterance pronounced in one breath. Both vowels are still heard in their purity, but they are pronounced in a gliding fashion, from one to the next.

In terms of intonation, Spanish tends to be "flatter" than English. Like English, though, declarative statements end with a slightly falling pitch. Questions tend to end with a slightly rising intonation, just as in English.

To get you pronouncing the Spanish phrases in this book as soon as possible and with a degree of accuracy that will enable you to be understood, there are only a handful of Spanish consonants and consonant combinations that require special attention from beginners. These are the letters **d**, **j**, **r**, the combination **rr**, the letters **b** and **v**, the combination **ll**, and the uniquely Spanish letter **ñ**:

- Whenever the letter **d** appears between vowels, it is softened to the sound of the English *th* as in the word *then*. In all other cases, it is pronounced as in the English word *dog*.
- The letter **j** is pronounced like an aspirated *h*, as in the *ch* in the surname *Bach*. It will be transcribed as an *h* in the pronunciation guide.
- Likewise, whenever the letter **r** appears between vowels, it is pronounced as the double consonants *tt* or *dd* are pronounced in the English words *rattle* or *paddle*. It is never pronounced as in the proper name *Ralph*.
- The double **rr** can be a challenge for English speakers. If you are familiar with the way the Scots roll their *r's*, then you know how it sounds. It takes some practice, but one way to begin is to place the tongue in the position to say the letter *d* just before the single Spanish *r* as explained above and try to say *el rey* or *un rey*.
- The letters **b** and **v** are pronounced in exactly the same way, but their pronunciation varies slightly depending on their position. The best approximation is achieved if you place your fingertip on your upper teeth and in a relaxed manner try to say the name

of the country *Cuba* (remembering the vowel **u** is pure, not as in *cube-uh*). You'll feel the air go around your fingertip and soften the hard, closed *b* sound. That is generally the way both the *b* and the *v* are pronounced, particularly when between vowels. When not between vowels, they are often pronounced as in the English word *boy*.

· In Mexico the double consonant **ll** is pronounced like the English letter *y*.

· The Spanish language is famous for its unique letter **ñ**. It is pronounced as in the middle of the English word *onion* and never as the letter *n*. Of course, Spanish also has a letter *n*, without the tilde. The simple *n is* pronounced the same as in English.

Just as in English, the letter **q** is followed by a **u**. It is pronounced like the letter *k*. The **u** is not pronounced when it follows the letter **q**, but the following vowel *is*. Thus, the word *¿Qué?* (What?) is pronounced *Kay*, like the woman's name, but without the glide into an *ee* sound as in English.

The phonetic transcriptions used in this guide are written so that if you pronounce them according to an American's way of reading them, with the few observations about vowels and the handful of consonants just described, you will be coming close enough to a native Mexican's pronunciation to be understood.

# Chapter 1

# Good Manners

 **Hola.** *(O-lah):* Hello.

This is a standard, everyday greeting you can use anywhere, anytime, with anyone. Of course, you will probably want to tailor your greeting to the time of day and also to the person you are addressing.

The respectful title of *señor* is often followed by the last name, if known. It translates as *sir* in terms of its degree of formality. Likewise, when addressing a woman, *señora,* the equivalent of *Mrs.*, or *ma'am,* is the proper form of address—if she is married. If she is unmarried, the form of address is *señorita,* the equivalent of *Miss.* Be careful when addressing women—some older women who have never been married are sensitive about being addressed as *señora,* often on moral grounds, based on religious scruples. Look for a wedding band if you are unsure. Do not use any of these titles of respect before a *first* name, because doing so can indicate a level of teasing or even sarcasm.

You can also customize your greeting for the time of day. The use of *señor, señora,* and *señorita* are optional and are included to show you how to incorporate them correctly.

| | |
|---|---|
| **Buenos días, señor.** | Good morning, sir. |
| BWEH-nos THEE-ahs sehn-YOR | |
| **Buenas tardes, señora.** | Good afternoon, ma'am. |
| BWEH-nahs TAHR-thehs sehn-YO-ra | |
| **Buenas noches, señorita.** | Good evening, miss. |
| BWEH-nahs NO-chehs sen-yo-REE-tah | |

**¿Cómo está usted?** *(KO-mo ehs-TAH oos-TEHD)*: How are you [singular]?

This is the way to ask someone how he or she is. It would logically follow the basic greetings above if a conversation were to continue. While English uses *you* for singular and plural and has no special form to show intimacy, Spanish has two forms of *you* in the singular. They are *tú* and *usted*. The *tú* form is used among family and close friends and should not be used instantly. Doing so indicates to the listener that the speaker is placing him- or herself in a superior social position. The moral of the story is that it is best to stick to *usted*. One may use the *tú* form on first meeting, but only when speaking to children and people clearly younger than the speaker.

| | |
|---|---|
| **Estoy bien, gracias. ¿Y usted?** | I am fine, thank you. And you? |
| ehs-TOY bee-yehn GRAH-see-yahs ee oos-TEHD | |
| **Estoy bien, gracias. ¿Y tú?** | I am fine, thank you. And you? |
| ehs-TOY bee-yehn GRAH-see-yahs ee TOO | |
| **¿Qué tal?** | How are things? |
| keh TAHL | |
| **Bien, gracias.** | Fine, thanks. |
| bee-yehn GRAH-see-yahs | |

**¿Cómo se llama usted?** *(KO-mo seh YAH-mah oos-TEHD):* What is your name?

This is the most frequently heard question for asking someone's name. In the reply, *me llamo* literally means *I call myself.* It means—or rather communicates—the same thing as the English expression. Remember that *usted* is the proper form of address for people you do not know and toward whom you wish to show common courtesy. As mentioned previously, one common exception to this general rule is that the *tú* form may be used when speaking with children and people who are *clearly* younger than the speaker.

| | |
|---|---|
| **¿Cómo te llamas?** | What is your name? |
| KO-mo teh YAH-mahs | |
| **Me llamo...** | My name is . . . |
| meh YAH-mo | |

 **Quiero presentarle a mi amigo/socio...** *(kee-EH-ro preh-sehn-TAR-leh ah mee ah-MEE-go/SO-see-o):* Allow me to introduce you to my friend/partner . . .

If you are traveling on business, it is likely that you will be introduced to people. This is what you will hear them say to you when they are taking you to meet a friend or business partner. The word *socio* is used strictly for a business partner, not a life partner. The literal meaning of *quiero* is *I want*; likewise, in the following sentence *me gustaría* means *it would please me* . . .

3

**Me gustaría presentarle a mi esposo/esposa/novio/novia.**
meh goos-tah-REE-ah preh-sen-TAHR-leh ah mee ehs-PO-so/ehs-PO-sah/NO-bee-o/NO-bee-ah

I would like to introduce you to my husband/wife/boyfriend/girlfriend.

**Mucho gusto en conocerle.** *(MOO-choh GUS-to ehn ko-no-SEHR-leh):* Pleasure to meet you.

After you have learned someone's name, either by asking him or her yourself or by having been introduced, it is polite to acknowledge one's satisfaction at having made his or her acquaintance. When a man is introduced to a woman, he may want to show his pleasure at meeting her and learning her name in a more gender-conscious manner and tell her he is charmed or enchanted to meet her. Likewise, a woman may wish to do the same when she has just learned a man's name. The two expressions below are a good way to begin to see, hear, and practice this distinction and they can be used rather often. It is not a good idea to use them when introduced to someone of the same sex. The use of this word isn't old-fashioned or strange in Spanish, even though it may sound over-the-top in modern American English.

**Encantado.**
ehn-kahn-TAH-tho

Enchanted. (male reply)

**Encantada.**
ehn-kahn-TAH-thah

Enchanted. (female reply)

**Igualmente.**
ee-gwahl-MEHN-teh

Likewise.

**¿Mande?** *(MAN-deh):* What did you say?

This is a phrase you will hear around you a great deal. It will probably be said to you as well. It is the uniquely Mexican way of asking someone to repeat what they just said. Literally, the word means "send" it again, only expressed as a question. In colloquial American English, the closest expression would be "Come again?" This is what you will probably need to say often, since much of the information you will hear will come at you faster than you can process it. Notice that the use of *no* before the verb makes the statement negative.

| | |
|---|---|
| **Hable más despacio, por favor.** | Speak more slowly, please. |
| AH-bleh mahs dehs-PAH-see-o por fa-BOR | |
| **No entiendo.** | I don't understand. |
| no ehn-tee-EHN-do | |

**Con permiso.** *(kon pehr-MEE-so):* Excuse me.

This phrase, and the others in this section, are what you will need in crowded places, because it is the thing to say to make your way through them. It is one you will hear Mexicans say quite often as they squeeze onto crowded buses or try to make their way among tables and chairs in restaurants.

You may hear them when someone is trying to get through or inviting you to move along in a line, enter an area, or when showing you which way to go. They are polite phrases to use if you wish to let someone go ahead of you, or if you need to move along. In any case, it is quite proper—expected, in fact—that after males reach a certain age, they should "let ladies go first." Chivalry is quite alive in daily manners in Mexico. By simply saying the statements with a question entonation (rising tone at the end of the phrase), you can also ask for directions or permission, as the case may be.

| | |
|---|---|
| **Pase usted.** | Come in./Go ahead./Keep going. |
| PAH-seh oos-TEHD | |
| **¿Puedo pasar/seguir?** | May I get through/go ahead? |
| PWEH-tho pah-SAHR/seh-GEER | |

**Disculpe.** *(dees-COOL-peh)*: Forgive me.

Literally, this means *forgive,* and while it is used when asking someone's forgiveness, (for which you should use *discúlpeme*), it is often used to get someone's attention when you might be interrupting them in some way.

| | |
|---|---|
| **Perdone.** | Pardon me. |
| pehr-DO-neh | |
| **Lo siento.** | I'm sorry. |
| loh see-EHN-to | |

**Pase usted.** *(PAH-seh oos-TEHD)*: Go ahead. After you.

This phrase is one you can use to be polite and allow someone to go ahead of you. It is proper in Mexico for men to observe some customs that have fallen out of fashion to some extent in the United States, such as letting a woman go ahead of them when both arrive at a door at the same time. This phrase is perfect for that.

**Adelante.**                                    Go ahead.
ah-deh-LAHN-teh

**Pare.**                                        Stop.
PAH-reh

🛫 **Adiós.** *(ah-thee-OS):* Good-bye.

Just as *hola* is a greeting you can use anytime, anywhere, and with anyone, *adiós* is the all-purpose way to say good-bye. At night, but not in the morning or afternoon, *adiós* may be preceded or followed by *buenas noches*. There are other ways to say good-bye that suggest when in the future or how far off into the future two people will meet again, or if they expect to. The phrase *vaya con Dios* (BAH-yah con THEE-os) somewhat familiar to English speakers because of a famous song, literally means *go with God* and is a form of leave-taking that implies that the person being said good-bye to is going on a long journey. A less religiously flavored version of that phrase—and a more festive one—is *buen viaje* (BWEHN bee-AH-heh), which means the same as the French expression we have adopted: *bon voyage*. When saying the following phrases, remember that the letter *h* is silent.

**Hasta pronto.**                                See you soon.
AHS-tah PRON-to

**Hasta luego.**                                 See you later.
AHS-tah loo-EH-go

**Hasta mañana.**                                See you tomorrow.
AHS-tah mah-nee-YA-nah

**Por favor.** *(por fah-BOR):* Please.

Manners are very important in Mexico and people do notice whether one has them or not. By having one or two common courtesy phrases on the tip of your tongue, you will see Mexican hospitality at its best. Beyond *please* and *thank you* there are a handful of other polite expressions that you will hear and should use. They are the social oil that makes interactions smooth and friendly in Mexico.

**Gracias.**          Thank you.
GRAH-see-ahs

**De nada.**          You're welcome.
deh NAH-thah

**No hay de qué.**          Think nothing of it.
no ay theh KEH

# Chapter 2

# Money

**¿Dónde puedo cambiar dinero?** *(DON-deh PWEH-tho kahm-bee-AHR dee-NEH-ro):* Where can I change money?

When planning your trip to Mexico, it is good to exchange a few dollars for pesos in a bank on this side of the border for taxis, tips, and a few incidental expenses. If you follow the exchange rates, you may or may not often obtain better exchange rates in Mexico than through your local bank or an airport currency exchange. In Mexico the best rates almost always can be found in banks or their ATMs. Since it can take some time to go through the line in a bank (sometimes more than one), you might consider going to one of the many *casas de cambio*, even though their rates are often a bit lower.

Banks and *casas de cambio*, as well as many shops in tourist areas, plainly post the exchange rates they are offering on a given day. Some shops in border areas or in places where there are a lot of tourists will accept U.S. dollars. You may see rates posted by some institutions or shop owners in a way that seems to confuse the comma with a decimal when writing numbers. This is not a mistake. It is normal. In fact, in most Spanish-speaking countries, the usage of commas and decimal points is the reverse of ours. You will likely see both formats in Mexico.

| | |
|---|---|
| **Quiero cambiar dólares por pesos.** | I want to change dollars for pesos. |
| kee-EH-ro kahm-bee-AHR DO-lah-rehs por PEH-sos | |

**¿A cómo está el dólar hoy?** *(ah KO-mo ehs-TAH ehl DO-lahr oy):* What's the dollar rate today?

Because all currencies tend to fluctuate in value with respect to each other, it is a good idea to keep your eye on the trends for a while before you travel. Changing or not changing your money on a particular day means gaining or losing purchasing power. You can lose—or gain—money by changing too much or too little, depending on the exchange rates. Be sure to have plenty of small bills for tips, meals, and other daily items for which using a credit card would be a bother. When you use a credit card, the issuer calculates your bill based on the exchange rate at the time of each purchase.

| | |
|---|---|
| **Está a diez punto treinta y ocho pesos por dólar.** | It's at 10.38 pesos per dollar. |
| ehs-TAH ah dee-EHS POON-to TRAYN-tah ee O-cho PEH-sos por DO-lahr | |
| **El dólar está fuerte/débil hoy.** | The dollar is strong/weak today. |
| ehl DO-lahr ehs-TAH FWEHR-teh/ THEH-beel oy | |

**Necesito billetes de a veinte.** *(neh-seh-SEE-to bee-YEH-tehs theh ah BEYN-teh):* I need twenty-peso bills.

Changing money, making change, and getting the size bills you want is easy if you know how to ask for bigger or smaller denominations. Familiarize yourself with the various Mexican bills and coins so you can count them at sight.

One interesting thing you'll see is the *escudo nacional,* or national seal, on the "tails" side of all coins. This is the famous eagle on the *nopal* cactus with a rattlesnake in its mouth. The image comes from a founding myth of the Nahuatl people (of which the Aztecs were one large nation). In this founding legend, a shaman had a dream in which it was revealed that they were to travel until they came to a place where they would see an eagle on a cactus with a snake in its mouth. There they were to found their city. That place was Tenochtitlán, now known as Mexico City.

| | |
|---|---|
| **Prefiero billetes de menor valor.** preh-fee-EH-ro bee-YEH-tehs theh meh-NOR ba-LOR | I prefer smaller bills. |
| **Déme billetes de mayor valor.** DEH-meh bee-YEH-tehs theh mah-YOR ba-LOR | Give me larger bills. |

**¿Cuánto desea usted cambiar?** *(KWAN-to deh-SEH-ah oos-TEHD kahm-bee-AHR):* How much do you wish to change?

It's never wise—in any country—to carry too much cash. Whether the risk you fear most is from pickpockets, your own absent-mindedness, or even just the wind and bad luck, you should only change as much as you need for a couple of days at a time. For carrying cash or other small valuables, it is wise to purchase a money belt. You can improvise a money belt in a pinch by getting any sort of pouch that you can attach to your belt and tuck into your pants, not in your pockets.

If your stay is lengthy and you are renting an apartment, it is likely that you'll prefer to change money less often, but you won't want to carry it around or open a bank account. What to do with your petty cash? There is one ingenious method for concealing larger amounts of cash if you are staying in an apartment. Obtain a few 35-mm photo canisters or plastic prescription pill bottles with the push-down-and-turn lids and roll bills into them. Use a screwdriver to remove the cover from electrical outlets, the more out of sight, the better (such as behind a sofa) and place the canister or pill bottles inside the wall. Don't hide all your cash in one outlet.

| | |
|---|---|
| **Quiero cambiar cien dólares.** | I want to change a hundred dollars. |
| kee-EH-ro kahm-bee-AHR see-EHN DO-lah-rehs | |
| **¿Tiene usted una calculadora que me pueda prestar?** | Do you have a calculator you can loan me? |
| tee-EH neh oos-TEH THOO-nah kal-koo-lah-THO-rah keh meh PWEH-theh pres-TAHR | |

**¿Puede usted cambiar este billete?** (*PWEH-theh oos-TEHD kahm-bee-AHR EHS-teh bee-YEH-teh*): Can you change this bill?

While you are in the process of getting dollars for pesos, it is a good idea to break them. Carrying large bills can be a problem because many small shop owners, taxi drivers, and even restaurants do not like to break large bills. If someone makes an error, remember that

Mexican culture avoids confrontation and direct blame, even over what Americans might consider small things. It is best to point to the error, not to the person who made it.

**Necesito cambio.**                    I need change.
neh-seh-SEE-to KAHM-bee-o

**El cambio no es correcto.**          The change is incorrect.
ehl KAHM-bee-o no-ehs ko-RREHK-to

**¿A qué hora se abre/se cierra el banco/la casa de cambio?**
*(ah KEH O-ra seh AH-breh/seh see-EH-rrah ehl BAHNG-ko/lah KAH-sah theh KAHM-bee-o):* What time does the bank/exchange open/close?

Hours of operation for banks and the *casas de cambio* are Monday through Friday. The posted hours begin between 9:30 and 10:30 A.M. and end between 11:00 A.M. and 1:00 P.M., so be sure you have either changed what you need for the weekend or can use credit cards or traveler's checks. The two largest Mexican banks are Banamex and Bancomer. In larger towns and cities these large banks are almost as common as Starbucks and their hours of operation are well observed. The *casas de cambio* can fudge a bit on opening and closing times, particularly the smaller operations. I recall one in Guadalajara near the Universidad Autónoma that sometimes would open or close a half hour earlier or later than the posted hours due to commuting difficulties.

13

✈ **¿Aceptan tarjetas de crédito?** *(ah-SEHP-tahn tahr-HEH-tahs deh KREH-dee-to):* Do you accept credit cards?

Nowadays, most businesses with a fixed storefront will accept credit cards. Most will accept traveler's checks as well. However, be prepared for the fact that most small vendors, such as those in open-air markets, will take only cash. Nowadays, with such widespread use of credit and debit cards, there is something almost romantic about using cash and going to these markets. In Mexico, depending on where you are, you may rediscover "real" money and letter writing—on real paper. The slower pace can be refreshing.

**¿Puedo pagar con cheques de viajero?**　　May I pay with traveler's checks?

PWEH-tho pah-GAHR kon CHEH-kehs theh bee-ah-HEH-ro

✈ **No traigo.** *(no TRAH-EE-go):* I don't have any (change).

Unfortunately, you will need this brief elliptical phrase more than you might wish—and not just for answering someone who might ask you to break a bill. It is the stock reply to beggars. Seeing small children begging in the streets is often a very uncomfortable situation for most visitors from the United States. Outright beggars abound in some areas, often indigenous women with their children. If you do give, you will be asked over and over again.

Children of the poorest families work in some way or another to help support themselves and their families. Children often as young as five or six years old can be seen selling *chicle* (CHEE-kleh) (chewing gum) in tiny packages that go for pennies a piece. By working and not outright begging, they preserve their dignity. My policy, and advice, is to buy a lot of gum, quietly and respectfully, even if you don't chew it.

**Puede guardar el cambio.**　　　You may keep the change.
PWEH-theh gwahr-DAHR ehl
　KAHM-bee-o

**¿Dónde está el cajero automático?** *(DON-deh ehs-TAH ehl ka-HEH-ro ah-o-to-MAH-tee-ko)*: Where is the ATM?

You can also opt for the more impersonal way of obtaining pesos at an ATM. As with any other credit card purchase at a retailer, the issuing bank will compute your bill based on the exchange rate at the time you make the withdrawal. Just as in the United States, it is a good idea, for security's sake, to use ATMs during the day, preferably in a crowded shopping mall, store, or in a bank. You might even practice using the Spanish prompts at your own bank in the United States or Canada!

**Sacar dinero**　　　To take out money
sah-KAHR dee-NEH-ro
**Contraseña**　　　Password
kon-trah-SEHN-yah

**¡La máquina me tragó la tarjeta!** *(lah MAH-kee-nah meh trah-GO lah tahr-HEH-tah)*: The machine ate my card!

Hopefully, you won't have to do any serious troubleshooting, but in the unlikely event that your card gets stuck in an ATM, you will need to be able to tell what happened. Finding a responsible person who is able to resolve the problem and get your card out may be the biggest problem. If it is after hours, you'll need to show up at the bank (best case scenario) as soon as they open the next day, to speak to the *gerente* (manager) about what happened *anoche* (ah-NO-cheh) (last night).

| | |
|---|---|
| **¿Puedo hablar con el gerente?** | May I speak with the manager? |
| PWEH-thoh ah-BLAHR ko nehl heh-REHN-teh | |
| **¿Cuándo van a poder sacar mi tarjeta?** | When will you be able to get my card out? |
| KWAHN-doh bah nah po-THEHR sah-KAHR mee tahr-HEH-tah | |

# Chapter 3

# Public Transportation

**Aquí tiene mi pasaporte.** *(ah-KEE tee-EH-neh mee pah-sah-POR-teh):* Here's my passport.

No matter how you enter Mexico, or how you leave, you will need to know how to answer a few questions and make your needs known. Besides simply performing the ticket-buying transaction (which you probably did on the U.S. or Canadian side), it is especially important to be able to identify members of your group or family as belonging together. This matters, not only when obtaining seat assignments, but also for the *aduaneros* (immigration officers) on both sides of the border.

If you are a parent traveling alone with your minor child or children, you will need to obtain a notarized affidavit, naming him, her, or them, that states that the other parent knows about the trip and gives permission for you to travel alone with the child or children. The same statement needs to authorize you to make any necessary medical decisions for the duration of the trip. Keep this affidavit with your passport.

If you are flying with a Mexican airline, you may want to request particular seat assignments. Even if you know the airline crew speaks English, at least well enough to do their jobs, using a little Spanish shows that you are making an effort—and Mexicans really appreciate that. Unlike the stereotype of the French, according to which foreigners are treated with disdain unless they speak French and speak it well, Mexicans feel honored when people try to speak their language.

| | |
|---|---|
| **Es mi hijo/hija.** | He/She is my son/daughter. |
| ehs mee EE-ho/EE-ha | |
| **Prefiero un asiento cerca de la** | I prefer a window/aisle seat. |
| **ventana/en el pasillo.** | |
| preh-fee-EH-ro oo nah-see-EHN-to | |
| SEHR-kah deh lah ben-TAH-na/ | |
| eh nehl pah-SEE-yo | |

**¿Puede llevarme al hotel...?** *(PWEH-theh yeh-BAHR-me ah lo-TEHL):* Can you take me to the . . . hotel?

After you arrive in Mexico, particularly by air, you will probably want to get to your hotel right away, if for no other reason that to relieve yourself of your luggage. If you are part of an organized tour, this leg of your journey may already be taken care of.

If not, do not worry: taxi service is plentiful, cheap, and reliable. Taxi travel in most cities is the best way to go. They usually operate from zones (*zonas,* also known as *colonias,* are roughly equivalent to neighborhoods). Taxis have stands where the taxi drivers congregate to wait for fares. A taxi stand is known as a *sitio* (literally, a place).

**¿Dónde está el sitio de taxis
  más cercano?**                   Where is the nearest taxi stand?
DON-theh ehs-TAH ehl SEE-tee-o
  theh TAK-sees mahs ser-KA-no

**¿Adónde quiere que lo lleve?**   Where do you want me to take you?
ah-THOHN-deh kee-EH-reh keh
  lo YEH-beh

**¿A cuánto me sale ir a...?** *(ah KWAHN-to meh SAH-leh eer
ah):* How much will it cost me to go to . . . ?

Once you've found a cab, be ready to negotiate. Of course, taxi drivers
will try to charge as much as they can get away with. Before you take
a taxi, ask someone at your hotel how much a reasonable fare would
be for the trip you plan to take. If you are reading this on the plane,
now is a good time to ask your flight attendant how much a reasonable fare would be from the airport to your hotel. Many cabbies also
are for hire at an hourly or a daily rate, in case you want or need them
for a series of errands.

Taxis in Mexico generally operate on a zone system. Taking a taxi
from the zone you are in to another destination outside your zone is
usually no problem, since the taxi you'll catch will be working from
the zone in which the trip originates. If the driver refuses, it is probably
because the zone you are going to is far away and he cannot return
with a fare. However, if you arrive at the *central de autobuses,* (sehn-
TRAHL theh aw-to-BOO-sehs) the main bus terminal in a downtown
area, and want to take a taxi to a particular neighborhood, you need
to find a taxi from that neighborhood. It's a turf issue. Likewise, cab
drivers who work from airports *may* also have zone preferences in

terms of where they are willing to go; therefore it is good to ask if they can take you where you want to go.

Usually the name of the zone from which a taxi operates will appear—*somewhere*—on the taxi. Standardized signage is another thing that is less common in Mexico as one opts for more economical forms of travel. Finally, always negotiate the price of the trip *before* you get in the cab. Literally, *before* you step into the cab. Getting in the cab constitutes an implied contract. If you have difficulty with numbers, have a pencil and paper handy so you and the cabbie can see, in writing, how many *pesos* the ride will cost.

| | |
|---|---|
| **¿Cuánto se cobra por zona?** | How much is it per zone? |
| KWAHN-to seh KO-brah por SO-nah | |
| **¿Cuánto cobra por hora/día?** | How much do you charge per hour/ |
| KWAHN-to KO-brah po-RO-ra/DEE-ah | day? |

 **Siga derecho/adelante.** *(SEE-gah theh-REH-cho/ah-theh-LAN-teh):* Go straight./Keep going.

Once you're in a taxi, if you *do* know where you are going, or if you really want the driver to go a particular route, it is important to be able to give directions. To make any of these commands negative, simply put *no* in front of them. Of course, these are also good phrases if you're going on foot. There are many forms of ground transportation, but taxis remain the best deal if getting directly to where you want to go is important. If not, the *colectivos* (ko-lehk-TEE-bos), a sort of public van pool that has a route with a set fare, will let you mingle with people and get to know the local spirit.

**Doble a la izquierda aquí.**      Turn left here.

DO-bleh a lah ees-kee-EHR-da ah-KEE

**Doble a la derecha en dos cuadras.**  Turn right in two blocks.

DO-bleh a lah theh-REH-chah

    ehn dos KWA-thrahs

**¿Pudiera usted mostrarme dónde estoy en el mapa?**

*(poo-dee-EH-rah oos-TEHD mos-TRAR-meh THON-deh ehs-TOY eh nehl MAH-pah):* Could you kindly show me where I am on the map?

Mexicans are known for being glad to give directions, even if they are not sure of them, because they consider it impolite not to try to help when asked. This can be very frustrating for foreigners until they become aware of this unwritten law of courtesy, illogical as it may seem. It takes a while before you can become good at reading their faces to see whether they are just trying to help or really know what they are saying.

One way to minimize unintentional misdirection is to show the person a map and ask them where you are on the map. Even if you already know, this tends to help even locals get their bearings, which could help prevent becoming more lost than you may already be.

Travel in Mexico, like Mexico herself, is quite varied. From 747s to mules, from ferryboats to anything that floats and can be called a boat, transportation is an adventure. Be prepared to roll with it when schedules or information on any form of transportation is not forthcoming. The only exception is air travel, particularly when it comes to international flights.

Mexico is a hardworking country with irregular infrastructure. That is one way to look at it. Airline employees at counters, flight attendants, and ticketing agents generally speak English reasonably well to very well. As you opt for more economical modes of travel, you will need to know more handy phrases.

It may seem impossible, but what was once Mexico's pride and joy, her railways, are no more. The most common and reliable forms of ground transportation are buses, taxis, or *colectivos*. They are plentiful, economical, and often fun—you meet real people. If you do drive your own car into Mexico, you will need to purchase Mexican automobile insurance before entering the country.

| | |
|---|---|
| **Favor de mostrarme cómo se llega a...** | Please show me how to get to . . . |
| fah-BOR deh mos-TRAHR-meh KO-mo seh YEH-gah ah | |
| **¿Dónde puedo comprar un mapa de la ciudad/de carreteras?** | Where can I buy a city/highway map? |
| DON-deh PWEH-thoh kom-PRAHR oom MAH-pah theh la see-oo-THAHD/theh kah-rreh-TEH-rahs | |

 **Permítame pasar.** *(pehr-MEE-tah-meh pah-SAHR):* Please let me through.

Mexicans in crowds, trying to get to a door, for instance, can be somewhat less concerned about orderly lines than are their neighbors to the north. A polite, yet somewhat determined, tone used when pronouncing this phrase might just help you keep from missing a plane, bus, or boat. The other expressions here can be turned into questions simply by using a question intonation (rising tone at the end of the phrase).

**Por aquí.**                          This way.
por ah-KEE
**Por allí.**                          That way.
por ah-YEE

✈ **¿Dónde está... ?** *(DON-theh ehs-TAH):* Where is . . . ?

This is probably one of the most important questions to learn to ask. Armed with a map, this question, and the answers—the directional vocabulary you saw earlier—you will find your way around like a pro. Of course, there are some common and logistically important places whose whereabouts you will need to know in order to make your travel more comfortable.

**¿Dónde está la línea aérea... ?**      Where is . . . airlines?
DON-theh ehs-TAH lah LEE-neh-ah
    ah-EH-reh-ah
**¿Dónde está la parada del**           Where is the bus stop?
    **autobús?**
DON-theh ehs-TAH lah pah-RAH-thah
    dehl ah-o-to-BOOS

✈ **¿Dónde se factura el equipaje?** *(DON-theh seh fahk-TOO-ra ehl eh-kee-PAH-heh):* Where do you check baggage?

Upon arrival at an airport, bus station, or cruise ship, you will travel more comfortably if you can leave your luggage in a secured area. Nowadays, this process is more streamlined because of security issues, but in some smaller operations you may need to find out a few things for yourself. You may also have to answer a few questions.

23

Remember that the only real questions have to do with security and service, and both involve being able to connect each bag with a traveler and his or her destination.

I have found that the most enjoyable times I have spent traveling in Mexico are the times when I had only carry-on baggage, like a duffle bag or a backpack. For today's world, add a laptop and you can share your trip via Internet from any of the plentiful Wi-Fi cafés that are springing up.

| | |
|---|---|
| **No tengo equipaje que facturar.** | I have no luggage to check. |
| no TEHNG-go eh-kee-PAH-heh | |
| ke fak-too-RAHR | |
| **Es mi portátil.** | It's my laptop. |
| ehs mee por-TAH-teel | |

**¿A qué hora llega/sale... ?** *(ah keh O-ra YEH-gah/ SAH-leh)*: What time does . . . arrive/leave?

Airline travelers and luxury cruise ship passengers need to know only a handful of useful phrases for times and places of arrival and departure. If you are already in Mexico and are awaiting the arrival or departure of other members of your party, coordinating with them often has to be done trusting in the information provided by transportation employees.

The rule of thumb about how much Spanish you need to know when traveling is that the simpler, more primitive or rural the mode of transportation, the more Spanish you need because the people around you will speak less and less English as the mode of travel becomes less sophisticated. But you can also have more fun, if you are not wedded to schedules. Travel in Mexico is part of the vacation.

**el vuelo**                                     the flight
ehl BWEH-lo

**el crucero de/para**                    the cruise ship from/bound for
ehl kroo-SEH-ro theh/PAH-ra

**He perdido mi boleto.** *(eh pehr-THEE-tho mee boh-LEH-to):* I have lost my ticket.

Next to the annoyance of not remembering if you've locked the front door or whether you've left the oven on, losing your ticket, or worrying about losing your ticket, is a sure way to have a bad time. The best way to avoid, or at least diminish, this worry is to keep a record of the *número/código de reservación* or *confirmación* (NOO-meh-ro/ KO-thee-go theh rreh-sehr-bah-see-ON)—reservation/confirmation number/code and the receipts *comprobantes* (kom-pro-BAHN-tehs) in a place separate from where you keep the tickets, preferably on your person. The same should be said of passports, which are now required for re-entry to the United States.

**Quiero cambiar mi boleto.**        I want to change my ticket.
kee-EH-ro kahm-bee-AHR mee
    boh-LEH-to

**¿Cuánto me cuesta cambiarlo?**    How much will it cost me to
KWAHN-to meh KWEHS-tah                change it?
    kahm-bee-AHR-lo

**Necesito arreglar transporte al aeropuerto.** *(neh-seh-SEE-to ah-rreh-GLAHR trahns-POR-teh ahl ay-ro-PWEHR-to):*
I need to arrange a ride to the airport.

They say that the Greek hero Ulysses learned more on his way home than he did on the outbound journey. Whether that is true of traveling to and from Mexico, I don't know, but the two processes seem to have their own quirks.

For one thing, going into Mexico you will probably note that the Mexican customs agents have fewer questions for you than the American ones will have for you as you, a returning citizen, try to come home. This is not a new phenomenon, but one that seems to have a more heightened sense of seriousness about it than a generation ago when the biggest question was whether you were carrying—shall we call it—contraband for personal use, or more bottles of tequila than allowed without paying duty.

**Tengo prisa.**
TEHNG-go PREE-sa

**Favor de guardar mi equipaje bajo llave hasta la hora de salida.**
fah-BOR deh GWAHR-dar mee
eh-kee-PAH-heh BAH-ho YA-beh
AHS-tah lah O-rah theh
sah-LEE-thah

I'm in a hurry.

Please store my luggage until it is time to go.

# Chapter 4

# Shopping

**Quisiera ver algo...** *(kee-see-EH-rah behr AHL-go):* I'd like to see something . . .

If a shop is busy, you may have to take the initiative to get service. The best way is to show interest in something, almost *anything* will do, so ending the line above with a sort of leading tone will direct the clerk toward where they think you are looking.

Most likely though, shopkeepers will approach you first, with the universal question "May I help you?": *¿En qué puedo servirle?* (ehng KEH PWEH-thoh sehr-BEER-leh). Naturally, it has a few variants. You, as a shopper, have a number of possible replies. You will rarely be asked this question in a U.S.-style grocery store unless you are wandering around and looking lost.

Shopkeepers have a unique culture. They survive by being attentive to clues that a person is interested in buying. Often there is more than one clerk in a privately owned store, which is likely a family operation. One adage among merchants is that no one enters the store who is not interested in buying—it's all a matter of getting the shopper to open up and talk so the merchant can direct or redirect his or her attention to an item that will fill a particular need.

I have noticed that Mexican shopkeepers are particularly astute at reading body language. They also have a system of gestures for communicating with each other about the various customers in a store so as not to waste time on some, to watch for potential shoplifters, or to zero in on an enthusiastic shopper and close a sale.

| | |
|---|---|
| **Busco un regalo/recuerdo.** | I'm looking for a gift/souvenir. |
| BOOS-ko oon rreh-GAH-lo/ rreh-KWEHR-do | |
| **Es para mi esposo/esposa.** | It's for my husband/wife. |
| ehs PAH-ra mee ehs-PO-so/ ehs-PO-sah | |

**Sólo estoy mirando, gracias.** *(SO-lo ehs-TOY mee-RAHN-do, GRAH-see-ahs):* I'm just looking, thanks.

This is the standard reply of shoppers who might be looking for something but are not ready to speak to a clerk. Of course, if you are serious about buying something, you'll need to be able to make your wishes known—and prepare to bargain if you are in a privately owned shop. After all, if you are looking for something and they have what you're looking for, everyone is happy, at least for the moment. Before asking about price, it is good to learn about the product so as to be able to begin bargaining from a knowledgeable position.

**¿De qué es?** *(deh KEH ehs)*: What is it made of?

When shopping for some items, you may want to know what something is made of. Likewise, if you are looking for something authentically Mexican, you want to be sure it is made in Mexico. Products made in Mexico are labeled *Hecho en México*. Educating yourself about products, even what they are made of, will place you in a better position to bargain because it will project an image to the clerk that you are not a spendthrift or naïve. Mexicans admire people who are sharp-witted. An innocent abroad is a mark for people inclined to take advantage of others.

 **No/Me gusta esto.** *(no/meh GOOS-tah EHS-to)*: I like/don't like this.

This is a standard phrase for expressing like or dislike. In a shopping context, this phrase helps the shopowner help you narrow your selection. For colors, "dark" and "light" are expressed by the name of the color followed by *oscuro* (os-KOO-ro) and *claro* (KLAH-ro), respectively. You can use three little words to indicate what you want, accompanied by pointing to individual items: *esto, eso,* and *aquello* (this one, that one, that one over there). These three little words are the verbal equivalents of pointing, so they are very valuable tools for making the objects of your interest known.

| | |
|---|---|
| **Prefiero esto/eso/aquello.**<br>preh-fee-EH-ro EHS-to/EH-so/<br>   ah-KEH-yo | I prefer this one/that one/that one<br>   over there. |
| **Es un poco grande/pequeño.**<br>ehs oom PO-ko GRAHN-deh/<br>   peh-KEHN-yo | It's a bit (too) large/small. |

**Necesito talla pequeña/mediana/grande.** *(neh-seh-SEE-to TAH-ya peh-KEHN-ya/meh-thee-AH-nah/GRAHN-deh):* I need a size small/medium/large.

Assuming you are in a clothing store, this generic statement has various permutations, depending on the sort of item you are looking for. Shoes, hats, gloves, and other such items are sized in centimeters, so it helps if you know in advance what items and sizes you, or someone you may shop for, use. Frequently, just a number is asked for, as in English. Fortunately, many clothes sold in the United States also have the metric size on the label, so you can know at least your own sizes rather quickly. Note that the word *talla* is *not* used for shoes, and since the word is feminine, the answer to it places *la* in front of the number that identifies the size. Likewise, *número* is masculine and so *el* is placed in front of the number that identifies the size.

**Calzo el (número) 42.**     I wear a size 42 shoe.
KAHL-soh ehl NOO-meh-ro
   kwah-REHN-tah ee dos
**Uso la (talla número) 39.**     I wear a size 39.
OO-so lah TAH-yah NOO-meh-ro
   TREYN-tah ee NWEH-beh

 **¿Cuánto cuesta esto?** *(KWAHN-to KWEHS-tah EHS-to):* How much is this?

Continuing the scenario in which you have found something you like and have learned something about it, now it's time to begin bargaining. Your initial inquiry will be the starting price for you to begin bidding downward. Some Americans are unused to bargaining except possibly at a car dealership or when buying a home. Many Americans are uncomfortable about haggling over the price of a shirt or a kilo of fresh mangos.

If you are not familiar with bargaining in an open-air market, the best way to look at it is as if the audience got to reverse roles with the auctioneer, who simply announces a starting price and sells when he can't afford to go lower.

**Creo que es una ganga.**               I think it's a bargain.
KREH-o keh eh-SOO-nah GAHNG-gah
**Lo siento, pero es demasiado.**       I'm sorry, but it's too expensive.
lo see-EHN-to PEH-ro ehs
   deh-mah-see-AH-thoh

**¿No me lo da en 5 pesos?** *(no meh lo dah ehn SEENG-ko PEH-sos):* Won't you give it to me for 5 pesos?

The art of bargaining, or *regateo* (reh-gah-TEH-o), is one you'll be able to practice, and should indulge in, at *mercados al aire libre* (mehr-KAH-do-sahl AY-reh LEE-breh), or open-air markets, or the indigenous version of the same, known as *tianguis* (tee-AHNG-ghees), and some small, privately owned retail stores, or *tiendas particulares* (tee-EHN-dahs pahr-tee-koo-LAH-rehs), where tourist items and *recuerdos* (reh-KWEHR-dos), or souvenirs, are sold. The finer points and strategies of verbal bargaining are too numerous to put in a brief guide, but with a bit of imagination you can often get as much as 20%–50% off, depending on the item and the mood of the shopkeeper.

During the negotiation process, it is very important never to show disrespect or disdain for an item. A poker face is better than any sort of expression to suggest the product is inferior. Mexicans tend to avoid direct conflict more than people in the United States. They are usually meticulously polite—so it is important to never let a rejection based on price seem to be an insult about their offer or the quality of their goods.

In other sorts of businesses operating from more fixed real estate, such as retail department stores in shopping malls, U.S.-style grocery stores, pharmacies, and so on, prices are marked and firm.

**¿Qué tal... pesos?**　　　　How about . . . pesos?
KEH tahl PEH-sos

**Muy bien, me lo llevo.**　　　Very well, I'll take it.
MOO-ee bee-EHN meh lo YEH-bo

**Gracias, voy a pensarlo.** *(GRAH-see-ahs BO ya pehn-SAHR-lo)*: Thanks, I'll think about it.

Whether your search was unsuccessful or you are playing a waiting game with the shopkeeper to see if he or she will drop the price as you appear to be leaving, it is good to end on a positive note. Thank the shopkeeper for his or her time. You may want to let them know somewhat indirectly that you will be doing some comparison shopping.

**Es lindo, pero voy a seguir**　　It's pretty, but I'm going to keep
**buscando.**　　　　　　　　looking.
ehs LEEN-do PEH-ro bo ya
　seh-GEER boos-KAN-do

**Tal vez regrese luego.**　　　I may come back later.
tahl behs rreh-GREH-seh loo-EH-go

**Busco...** *(BOOS-ko):* I'm looking for . . .

Finally, some comments on vocabulary. When you can name the item you are looking for you'll find it a lot faster. Some general categories are listed below. If you are going to shop seriously, it is a good idea to look up all the names of the things you want to buy so you can finish the preceding sample sentence. That might not be your style. So, another way to acquire vocabulary on the go is to read the labels of items that are obvious. For instance, if you see a bottle of juice labeled *jugo de naranja,* you can probably see that it is orange juice—it probably also has a picture of an orange on it to confirm your suspicion. A trip to a grocery store or a pharmacy will teach you a lot of vocabulary.

**ropa/playeras/camisetas/traje
  de baño**
RRO-pa/plah-YEH-rahs/kah-mee-
  SEH-tahs/TRAH-heh theh BAHN-yo

clothes/beachware/T-shirts/
  bathing suit

**una farmacia/loción protectora/
  aspirina**
OO-nah fahr-MAH-see-ah/lo-see-ON
  pro-tehk-TO-ra/ahs-pee-REE-nah

a pharmacy/suntan lotion/aspirin

**joyas/sortijas/aretes/pulseras/
  relojes**
HO-yahs/sor-TEE-hahs/ah-REH-tehs/
  pool-SEH-rahs/rreh-LO-hehs

jewelry/rings/earrings/bracelets/
  watches

**objetos de arte/artesanía**
ob-HEH-tos theh AHR-teh/
  ahr-teh-sah-NEE-ah

art objects/crafts

**Qué pena que no lo manejen.** *(keh PEH-nah keh no lo mah-NEH-hen):* What a shame you don't carry that.

You've found out, or figured out, that the shop doesn't carry what you're looking for. Even if you think you've hit a dead end, you might be able to get information from the clerk. He or she may be able to tell you where you can get the item or service you are looking for. Naturally, if a shopowner doesn't carry an item, telling you where you can find it is not considered helping competition. Once again, you'll generally see Mexican hospitality and helpfulness when you ask for help, unless the store is extremely busy.

| | |
|---|---|
| **¿Dónde puedo conseguirlo?** | Where can I find it? |
| DON-deh PWEH-thoh kon-seh-GEER-lo | |
| **Voy a buscarlo allí, gracias.** | I'll go look for it there, thanks. |
| BO-ya boos-KAR-lo ah-YEE, GRAH-see-ahs | |

# Chapter 5

# Shopping for Food

**¡Qué frescas se ven estas frutas!** *(keh FREHS-kas seh ben EHS-tahs FROO-tahs):* How fresh this fruit looks!

Vendors are always eager to sell, and showing enthusiasm for their products is a good way to attract their attention and get good service. A few handy phrases about describing fruits and vegetables will enable you to get the items you want.

In a busy market, especially an open-air food market, you sometimes need to elbow past the eager local shoppers, who have several advantages over you! The right phrase will get the ear of the owner. Just as one will hear *¿En qué puedo servirle?* (ehn KEH PWEH-tho sehr-VEER-leh) in shops and even at a fruit stand, one may hear *¿Qué le damos, señor?* (keh leh THA-mos sehn-YOR) in places where edibles, or *comestibles* (ko-mehs-TEE-blehs), are sold, especially in open-air markets. This phrase is comparable to the English phrases heard in a farmer's market "What'll it be for you today?" or "What can I get for you?" One possible reply, if you are genuinely interested in entering into the bartering mode, is the first phrase on the next page. It amounts to a counter-question, inviting the vendor to show you what he or she has on sale or as a specialty item. It literally means "What is being offered to me?" If you are not in a bartering mood, you can politely let the vendor know so he or she does not focus on you, but on other customers. When you're in this frame of mind you should stick to the U.S.-style markets, or you will almost certainly be overpaying.

| | |
|---|---|
| **¿Qué se me ofrece?** | What are you offering? |
| keh seh me o-FREH-seh | |
| **Nada, pues, gracias.** | Nothing, really, thanks. |
| NAH-thah pwehs GRAH-see-ahs | |

**¿Me permite probar los cacahuates?** *(meh pehr-MEE-teh pro-BAHR los kah-kah-WHAH-tehs)*: May I sample the peanuts?

It is perfectly permissible to sample many food items in the open-air markets, but unless the stallkeeper is actually offering, it is proper to ask permission. You may find that the names of many fruits and vegetables are not Spanish, but rather come from indigenous languages, often Náhuatl, the language of the Aztecs. Sometimes this is because the Spanish name never caught on or, more interestingly, because the product is native to Mexico. Some may find it interesting to know that many agricultural products now used the world over are from the Americas, many of them from Mexico: *cacahuates* (kah-kah-WHAH-tehs) peanuts, *maíz* (mah-EEZ) corn, *chocolate* (cho-ko-LAH-teh) chocolate, *jitomates* (hee-to-MAH-tehs) tomatoes, *papas* (PAH-pahs) potatoes, and *camotes* (kah-MO-tehs) sweet potatoes, to name just a few. Personally, I find it validating to know that *Xocolatl* (originally pronounced sho-ko-LAH-TL) was a god!

If a vendor is holding something out for you to taste, he or she may invite you to try it by simply saying *¿Gustas?* (GOOS-tahs). If a tray is used to display samples, for politeness' sake, you might ask to try them—or something else.

| | |
|---|---|
| **Me gustaría probar esto.** | I'd like to try this. |
| meh goos-tah-REE-ah pro-BAHR EHS-to | |
| **¿Me permite?** | May I? |
| meh pehr-MEE-teh | |

**¡Qué rico!** *(keh RREE-ko):* How delicious!

You may have a little difficulty remembering whether to say *rico, rica, ricos,* or *ricas,* but when you are offered an item, or items, *listen* to whether you were invited to try them by being told *pruébelo* or *pruébela,* and so on, and you'll be on target. Even if you're not, *¡qué rico!* (keh RREE-ko) will always do.

When sampling food, remember that for Mexicans, food is very special. To eat with someone is to show some degree of trust. Consider the Spanish word for companion: *compañero.* The root word is *pan,* meaning *bread.* The prefix *con* means *with*—thus, a *companion* is *someone with whom you break bread.* The root meaning of this word still resonates in Spanish-speaking cultures. The bottom line is: always show respect for the food you are served—it is an extension of the person who made it or who is sharing it with you.

| | |
|---|---|
| **¡Me encanta esto!** | I love this! |
| mehng-KAN-tah EHS-to | |
| **¡Maravilloso!** | Marvellous! |
| mah-rah-bee-YO-so | |

✈ **Éstas están maduras, ¿no?** *(EHS-tah sehs-TAHN mah-THOO-rahs no):* These are ripe, aren't they?

It never hurts to confirm the ripeness or readiness of a fruit one more time before you seal a deal—particularly if you are trying a *new* fruit. There is much to try in Mexico that is not commonly found in U.S. grocery stores, although some unusual items are making their way to the higher-end grocers. Some examples include *pitahayas*—known in English as *dragonfruit*—that comes in different colors. Another is *cherimoya,* a fruit that is known by the same name in English and looks a little like an artichoke. To the uninitiated, they look, well, inedible, until you see the luscious flesh inside.

| | |
|---|---|
| **¿Cómo se sirve esto?** | How does one serve this? |
| KO-mo seh SEER-behs-to | |
| **Está/Están verde/s todavía.** | It is /they are still green. |
| ehs-TAH/ehs-TAHN BEHR-dehs | |
|    to-thah-BEE-ah | |

✈ **¿Cuánto cuesta un kilo de esto?** *(KWAHN-to KWEHS-tah oong KEE-lo theh EHS-to):* How much does a kilo of this cost?

Brush up on your metric system equivalents along with learning the phrases in this section if you should need to buy fruits, vegetables, or meats. Roughly speaking, a *medio kilo* (MEH-dee-o KEE-lo), or half a kilo, is a little over a pound, and a *cuarto* (KWAHR-to) is a bit over a half a pound.

Whether in the supermarkets, with their *precios fijos* (PREH-see-os FEE-hos), or set prices, or in the open-air markets, where you can haggle, you'll need to adjust how you calculate amounts you need for cooking your favorite recipes if you plan to do much food preparation in Mexico. Buying fruit for breakfast or snacks is an uncomplicated and rather pleasant affair if you find yourself near an open-air market. One interesting linguistic fact is that if you ask for a lemon and say only *limón*, you will get a lime, unless you ask for *un limón amarillo* (oon lee-MON ah-mah-REE-yo), literally, a *yellow lime*. Note that one may use *por, el,* or *la* in front of a weight or measure, with the meaning of *per*.

**¿A cuánto el kilo?**  How much per kilo?
ah KWAHN-to ehl KEE-lo

**¿A cuánto la mano?**  How much per bunch (handful)?
ah KWAHN-to lah MA-no

**Déme medio kilo de jitomates.** *(DEH-me MEH-dee-o KEE-lo theh hee-to-MAH-tehs):* Give me a half kilo of tomatoes.

Unlike the United States, Mexico has modernized—or internationalized—by being on the metric system. A kilo is 2.2 pounds, so if you need to do some fast calculating in your head, a pound is roughly half a kilo. The standard expression for ordering is to say *Déme...* (Give me . . . ). If you have been in a market where bargaining is expected, be sure you have settled on the price per unit or by weight before they begin loading the scale. Just as getting in a taxi is an implied contract to pay what the driver will later tell you, the act of loading the scale is an implied contract to purchase.

**Quisiera media docena de aguacates.**

kee-see-EH-ra MEH-dee-ah thoh-SEH-nah theh ah-gwah-KAH-tehs

I'd like half a dozen avocados.

**Me gustaría comprar cinco plátanos.**

meh goos-tah-REE-a kom-PRAHR SEENG-ko PLAH-tah-nos

I'd like to buy five bananas.

**¡Ya, cabal!** *(YAH kah-BAHL):* That's it!

In many open-air markets, as soon as you have indicated how much of something you want, you may see the vendor weigh your order—often on a makeshift scale—and declare *¡ya, cabal!*, when the desired weight is reached. This roughly translates as *full* (or *complete*) *already!* At that time, the vendor will probably announce the final price or ask if you need anything more. If you don't understand the numbers quickly enough, have a pencil and paper ready for him or her to write down the amount so there is no confusion or misunderstanding—something Mexicans really make an art of avoiding.

**Necesito algo más.**

neh-seh-SEE-to AHL-go mahs

I need something else.

**Es todo, gracias.**

ehs TO-tho GRAH-see-ahs

That's it, thanks.

🛫 **¿Manejan comida para bebés?** *(mah-NEH-hahn ko-MEE-thah PAH-rah beh-BEHS):* Do you carry baby food?

The best, most reliable source for packaged baby food and formula is in a national chain grocery store where you can find equivalents to what you buy in the United States or Canada. When feeding babies adult foods which you might buy in an open-air market, be sure the skin of fruit is unbroken and that you properly sanitize it before cutting it. Bananas are a great thing to have on hand if your baby likes them. Note that fresh apples and grapes are expensive because they are not grown extensively in Mexico. Mexico imports most of its apples from Washington state.

| | |
|---|---|
| **¿Manejan botellas para bebés?** | Do you carry baby bottles? |
| mah-NEH-hahn bo-TEH-yahs | |
|    PAH-rah beh-BEHS | |
| **Necesito comprar pañales** | I need to buy disposable diapers. |
|    **desechables.** | |
| Neh-seh-SEE-to kom-PRAHR | |
|    pahn-YAH-lehs deh-seh-CHA-blehs | |

🛫 **¿Hay un lugar aquí con frutas y verduras orgánicas?** *(ah-YOON loo-GAHR ah-KEE kon FROO-tah see behr-DOO-rah sor-GAH-nee-kahs):* Is there a place here with organic fruits and vegetables?

There are a lot of organic farms in Mexico, as a trip to your own local supermarket in the United States or Canada will prove. If you are absolutely determined to find certified organic food, you will do better at the very large, U.S.-style supermarkets. Given the increasing popularity of organics, here and in Mexico, it is ever more likely, especially in

41

areas where there are many tourists, that you will find organic food vendors in a farmer's market. When making requests, don't forget to add *por favor* and to thank the person with *gracias*.

| | |
|---|---|
| **¿Tiene pesticidas/herbicidas?** | Does it have pesticides/herbicides? |
| tee-EH-neh pehs-tee-SEE-thahs/ | |
| her-bee-SEE-thahs | |
| **¿Dónde está la lista de** | Where is the list of ingredients? |
| **ingredientes?** | |
| DON-deh ehs-TAH lah LEES-tah theh | |
| eeng-greh-thee-EHN-tehs | |

 **Soy vegetariano/na.** *(soy beh-heh-tah-ree-AH-no/nah):* I am a vegetarian.

If you have special dietary needs, for whatever reason, you should look up the particular foods you can eat as well as those you do not. It also is advisable to know the Spanish term for any condition you may have. See Chapter 12, Health Issues, and Chapter 13, Emergencies, for more vocabulary.

| | |
|---|---|
| **No puedo comer productos** | I cannot eat milk products. |
| **lácteos.** | |
| no PWEH-tho ko-MEHR pro- | |
| DOOK-tos LAHK-teh-os | |
| **No puedo comer productos** | I cannot eat wheat products. |
| **de trigo.** | |
| no PWEH-tho ko-MEHR pro- | |
| DOOK-tos de TREE-go | |

# Chapter 6

# Friendship and Romance

**Tutéame, por favor.** *(too-TEH-ah-meh por fah-BOR):* Let's be on a first-name basis, please.

If you happen to make a friend in Mexico, at some point you may wish to address him or her in an informal, friendly way. This is when you stop using the formal *usted* forms with a title and start using the *tú* forms along with your friend's first name. You may initiate the use of the *tú* form even if it is clear that your Spanish is not nearly good enough to really allow you to use the verb forms. It is the gesture that communicates the friendship. Delicate as the situation is, if it is very clear that the person is warming up to you, it is probably permissible to invite the informal form of *tú*. In English, the only close equivalent is that of being on a *first-name basis*.

If a Spanish speaker invites you to use the familiar form of address, the invitation should *never* be interpreted as a cue or invitation to become romantically involved. It simply is an invitation to be less formal, to have a more relaxed relationship. Just when that happens is going to vary widely and depends on many factors. There are a couple of ways you may invite someone (or someone may invite you) to be on a less formal, or even friendship, basis with someone.

| | |
|---|---|
| **Podemos tutearnos.** | We can use the *tú* form with each |
| po-THEH-mos too-teh-AHR-nos | other. |
| **Vamos a tutearnos.** | Let's use *tú* with each other. |
| BAH-mo sah too-teh-AHR-nos | |

**Gracias, eres muy amable.** (*GRAH-see-ahs EH-rehs MOO-ee ah-MAH-bleh*): Thanks. You are very nice.

Obviously, the person invited to be less formal will say thank you. If you do manage to become this friendly with someone, it is likely—no, it is certain—that you will need to know more about the culture, and certainly more Spanish than can be offered here. However, it must be said that Mexicans have a somewhat suspicious view of Americans offering friendship because we tend to use the word "friend" when really the person is a mere acquaintance. In Mexico, indeed in most of the Latin world, friendship is earned and cherished. An invitation to lunch is not a casual thing. Holidays, birthdays, and other events just don't seem right without including all who fall in that inner circle.

| | |
|---|---|
| **Gracias, usar *usted* es muy formal.** | Thanks, using *usted* is very formal. |
| GRAH-see-ahs oo-SAHR oos-TEHD ehs MOO-ee for-MAHL | |
| **Gracias, me alegro de ser tu amigo/amiga.** | Thanks, I'm glad to be your (male/female) friend. |
| GRAH-see-ahs meh ah-LEH-gro theh sehr too ah-MEE-go/ah-MEE-gah | |

**Tú me caes bien.** *(too meh KAH-ehs bee-EHN):* You are very likeable.

This colloquial expression literally translates as *you fall on me well*, but it is meant in terms of the impression one makes on another person. Of course, one could also say *me caes mal* (meh kah-ehs MAHL), which would be insulting. There are many ways to express one's liking or dislike for people and the more playful ones are great among friends.

Don't be surprised if a Mexican friend decides to bestow a nickname on you. This is a good thing—a sign that you are memorable in some good way. There is no sure way to know what that nickname will be. Many choices have to do with translating your name into Spanish and using the Spanish nickname for that name, such as Paco, which is the short form of Francisco, the Spanish version of Frank. But don't be surprised if it is something that refers to a physical trait, something akin to a verbal caricature. If you have a light complexion, one common nickname, almost a generic or fall-back choice, is *güero* or *güera* (GWEH-ro/GWEH-rah), or *blondie*! Even if you don't like it, accept it.

| | |
|---|---|
| **Eres buena onda.** | You're cool. |
| EH-rehs BWEH-nah ON-dah | |
| **Creo que vamos a llevarnos bien.** | I think we're going to get along well. |
| KREH-o keh BA-mo sah yeh- | |
|    BAHR-nos bee-EHN | |

**¿Me acompañas?** *(meh ah-kom-PAHN-yas):* Will you go with me?

Once a relationship is on a *tú* basis, it could be appropriate to make the almost universal social gesture of inviting someone to dinner or some other similar setting where food is served. Remember that if you invite someone, or if you invite a group, you are expected to pay. There is no fighting over the tab to impress people! If you are in a group and invite one person, it may well be interpreted as an invitation to the group. While we say "going Dutch" or "Dutch date" to indicate that each person is paying his or her own way, this is looked down upon in Mexico and is known as (are you ready?) going *a la americana* (referring to the United States).

Note the difference between *una bebida* (OO-nah beh-BEE-thah), an alcoholic beverage, and *un refresco* (oon rreh-FREHS-ko), a term that includes soft drinks and other non-alcoholic drinks.

| | |
|---|---|
| **¿Quisieras cenar conmigo?** | Would you like to have dinner |
| kee-see-EH-rahs seh-NAHR | with me? |
| kon-MEE-go | |
| **¿Quieres un refresco?** | Would you care for a soda? |
| kee-EH-rehs oon rreh-FREHS-ko | |

**¿Qué tomas?** *(keh TO-mahs):* What are you drinking?

This phrase also means *What do you drink?*, but in the context of a nightclub or bar it means *What are you having right now?* Remember, *quien invita, paga* (he/she who invites, pays).

The word *trago* implies some form of hard liquor, anything from a mixed drink to a shot, but is often used casually to invite someone to have something stronger than soda. While drinking habits vary among Mexicans as much as they do among Americans, most Mexicans, men and women, do drink socially, even if only a sip. Temperance leagues never made significant inroads south of the border. That said, drinking to excess is generally looked down upon, particularly among the well-to-do—at least when in mixed company. A group of men of nearly every social class will occasionally overindulge.

**Te invito a tomar un trago.**                    Have a drink with me.

teh eem-BEE-to ah to-MAHR

    oon TRAH-go

**¿Prefieres una cerveza u**                    Do you prefer beer or some other

    **otra bebida?**                    drink?

preh-fee-EH-rehs OO-nah sehr-BEH-

    sah oo O-trah beh-BEE-dah

      **Quiero invitarte a...** *(kee-EH-ro eem-bee-TAHR-te ah):*
I want to invite you to . . .

This short phrase is easy to complete. You can fill in the blank with a
verb form as found in a dictionary. They end in *-ar, -er,* or *-ir,* such
as *nadar, comer,* or *ir* (to swim, to eat, or to go). Or you can fill in the blank
with a noun, such as *una fiesta* (a party) or *la playa* (the beach). This is
a great phrase because it is quite literally "plug-and-play," since you
can put in any verb or noun that makes sense to complete the idea
of inviting someone to do something or to go somewhere. Of course,
you can ask open-ended questions to find out what the other person
might like to do—always a good idea! If you think you'll be in this linguistic territory, it might be a good idea to look up the Spanish names
of the sports or hobbies you enjoy.

**¿Qué te gusta hacer en el tiempo**       What do you like to do in your

    **libre?**                    free time?

keh teh GOOS-tah ah-SEHR eh nehl

    tee-EHM-po LEE-breh

**¿Qué prefieres hacer ahora?**       What would you prefer to do now?

keh preh-fee-EH-rehs ah-SEHR

    ah-O-rah

**¿Adónde vamos mañana/esta noche?** *(ah-THOHN-deh BAH-mos mahn-YAH-nah/EHS-tah NOH-cheh):* Where do you want to go tomorrow/tonight?

This is a gentle way of asking someone to go out with you. Naturally, you may be the one invited, so it is good to recognize this expression as well as be able to use it yourself. As in English-speaking countries, traditionally the man is the one who makes the invitation. Therefore, it is more likely that male readers will be the ones using this expression and women will need to recognize it and answer it appropriately. This rule tends to be more true than not in Mexico, even among the more affluent. Among the less affluent, the more such old-fashioned formalities are strictly observed.

| | |
|---|---|
| **Te espero en dos horas.** | I'll wait for you in two hours. |
| Teh ehs-PEH-ro ehn dos O-rahs | |
| **¿Dónde quieres que te espere?** | Where do you want me to wait |
| DON-deh kee-EH-rehs keh teh | for you? |
| ehs-PEH-reh | |

 **Puedo ir a buscarte a las seis**. *(PWEH-tho ee rah boos-KAHR-teh ah lah seys):* I can come by for you at six.

A good way to firm up plans is to propose something definitive. If you wish to indicate your availability, you might ask *Could you come by for me at six?,* that is, *¿Puedes buscarme a las seis?* (PWEH-thes boos-KAHR-me ah lah seys). The risk of seeming too available is, of course, a possibility. In fact, there is a proverb that sums up the dilemma for women: *La mujer debe ser hallada, pero tan hallada, no* (A woman should be available, but not too much so).

Finally, remember that in Mexico, indeed in most Latin countries, being fashionably late is still a common practice and social life may not begin until after many English speakers have gone to bed!

**Te encuentro enfrente del hotel.**     I'll meet you in front of the hotel.
teh ehn-KWEHN-tro ehm-FREHN-teh
    dehl o-TEHL

**Esta noche, no. ¿Qué tal mañana?**     Not tonight. How about tomorrow?
EHS-tah NO-cheh no keh tahl
    mahn-YAH-nah

 **Eres muy linda.** *(EH-rehs MOO-ee LEEN-dah)*: You're very pretty.

In a dating situation, or one that seems to be headed that way, a few complimentary phrases are always helpful. Note that the adjectives ending in -*a* are in statements directed at a female, while those ending in -*o* are in phrases directed at a male. The difference between the first and second statements below is due to the choice of the verbs *ser* or *estar*. In the second phrase, the speaker is complimenting a woman on how beautiful she has made herself for the evening. In the first, the man speaking is telling her how truly beautiful she is—regardless of circumstance!

**¡Qué guapa eres!**          How beautiful you are!
keh GWAH-pah EH-rehs

**¡Qué guapa estás!**          How beautiful you look!
keh GWAH-pah ehs-TAHS

**¡Ay, qué guapo!**          Wow, how handsome!
AH-ee keh GWAH-po

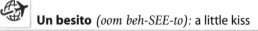 **Un besito** *(oom beh-SEE-to):* a little kiss

At the end of a good evening, a romantic kiss on a first date is *not* a good idea. A peck on the cheek and a hug is often reasonable and appropriate. In fact, men should not be surprised if they ask a woman out, she accepts, and he finds himself paying for three instead of two. Chaperoned dates are a way of life for many respectable young women in Mexico, if they still live at home. Men of almost any age may be told flat out by a woman of marrying age that before she can go out with him, he will have to meet her family. Many young people continue to live at home until they marry, but this is not always the case among young professionals living in urban areas.

| | |
|---|---|
| **un abrazo** | a hug |
| oo nah-BRAH-so | |
| **Tus ojos son muy lindos.** | Your eyes are beautiful. |
| too SO-hos son MOO-ee LEEN-dos | |

 **Lo he pasado muy bien contigo.** *(lo eh pah-SAH-tho MOO-ee bee-EHN kon-TEE-go):* I've had a nice time with you.

If all goes well and you would like to see the person again, and keep up with him or her, you need to know how to keep the lines of communication open. Reciprocity is the rule, of course. Nowadays, this is much easier than in the past.

Still, having to say good-bye to someone with whom you feel there are serious possibilities of romance is difficult in any cultural setting. If you find yourself in such a situation, having some sort of going-away party, known as *una fiesta de despedida,* is a must, at which it is important to make your intentions clear and publicly known.

**¿Cuál es tu número de teléfono?**     What is your phone number?

KWAH-lehs too NOO-meh-ro theh
   teh-LEH-fo-no

**¿Tienes correo electrónico?**     Do you have e-mail?

tee-EH-nehs ko-RREH-o eh-lehk-
   TRO-nee-ko

# Chapter 7

# Hotels

**Tengo una reservación para dos.** *(TEHNG-go OO-nah rreh-sehr-bah-see-ON PAH-rah dos):* I have a reservation for two.

If you are a backpacking tourist—the footloose and fancy-free sort—you will probably not make reservations but rely on your wits or guidebooks. Those less inclined to serendipity—families and most couples—will want to make reservations in upscale hotels and resorts. Getting checked in is a smooth process in hotels that accept reservations in the United States or Canada. You still will need to provide information for billing and so forth before you can go to your room to relax and recuperate from your travels.

| | |
|---|---|
| **La hice por correo electrónico.** lah EE-seh por ko-RREH-o eh-lek-TRO-ni-ko | I made it by e-mail. |
| **Reservé el cuarto con mi tarjeta de crédito.** rreh-sehr-BEH ehl KWAHR-to kon mee tahr-HEH-tah theh KREH-dee-to | I reserved my room with my credit card. |

**Queremos quedarnos dos noches, no más.** *(keh-REH-mos keh-DAHR-nos dos NO-chehs no mahs):* We just want to stay two nights.

Mexican hospitality is relaxed, unhurried, and genuinely warm. It is one of the country's points of patriotic pride. Patience and graciousness are the keys to resolving any confusion. As long as you have a confirmation, you can almost always count on a good stay from a service point of view. Depending on the type of hotel you are in, there will be more or fewer problems to resolve.

In hotels where reservations are not necessary, count on some problems not being perceived as problems (most often involving plumbing). For example, as has happened to me often enough to report, if you are traveling to a coastal town, say, to go deep-sea fishing, consider any last-minute accommodations as camping expeditions. You might consider packing your own supply of toilet paper or a fresh towel if you plan to travel without reservations. Despite some inconveniences, the staff in such places are as genuine as you'll find in the most expensive places. For instance, in one less-than-up-to-code hotel, I played cards one night with the front-desk clerks who, without fanfare, provided cold beer on the house, just because a *gringo* was friendly enough to hang out and talk.

| | |
|---|---|
| **¿Tienen un cuarto disponible para dos?** | Do you have any rooms available for two? |
| tee-EH-nehn oon KWAHR-to dees-po-NEE-bleh PAH-ra dos | |
| **Quisiéramos dos llaves, por favor.** | We would like two keys, please. |
| kee-see-EH-rah-mos dos YA-behs por fah-BOR | |

**Póngame con el servicio al cuarto, por favor.** *(PONG-gah-meh ko nehl sehr-BEE-see-o ahl KWAHR-to por fah-BOR):* Connect me to room service, please.

Naturally, in luxury resorts and other multi-starred accommodations, you'll be able to get room service. In many of the sorts of hotels where middle-class Mexicans stay when they venture, for instance, from the megalopolis of Mexico City to the beach for a weekend or a few days with their families, accommodations may not include any room service or even a restaurant in the hotel. In some smaller hotels you may find that water is dispensed by tipping a rocking chair placed in a common area, into which is tied a ten-liter glass jug with a large cork in the top. If you mistrust the safety of this system, buy bottled water, *agua mineral* (AH-gwah mee-neh-RAHL), in a local store.

So, once in your room, if you're hungry, you may need to make a few inquiries about local eateries and other services that larger hotels offer as part of their hospitality. Whenever you have any room service, or even for the hotel maid service, it is a good idea to leave some sort of tip. You could write a short note saying "Propina" (pro-PEE-nah) or "Gracias por su servicio" (GRAH-see-ahs por soo sehr-BEE-see-o) and leave it in a visible place, such as on the bathroom counter or in the middle of the bed. It's a small touch, but it can go a long way if you need a little extra help with something else during your stay.

**¿Cuáles son las horas de servicio al cuarto?**
KWAH-leh-son lah SOH-rahs de sehr-BEE-see-o ahl KWAHR-to

What hours is room service available?

**Quisiera desayunar/almorzar en mi cuarto.**
kee-see-EH-rah dehs-ah-yoo-NAHR/ ahl-mor-SAHR ehn mee KWAHR-to

I'd like to have breakfast/lunch in my room.

**Necesito más toallas/sábanas limpias.** *(neh-seh-SEE-to mahs to-AH-yahs/SAH-bah-nahs LEEM-pee-ahs):* I need more towels/clean sheets.

When something doesn't work in a luxury hotel, you're likely to get attention about as quickly as you would in similar accommodations in the United States or Canada. However, in more "local" establishments it can take awhile. Some of the easiest things to get are towels and linens. Some of the more cumbersome problems, just as here, include plumbing or electrical problems.

Sometimes, it doesn't hurt—and it may be necessary—to ask for a different room. Other times, it helps to be able to just point to a complicated problem, but you'll need to have the hotel staff come to your room.

**El televisor/el teléfono/ la regadera no funciona.**
ehl teh-leh-bee-SOR/ehl teh-LEH-fo-no/lah rreh-gah-DEH-ra no foon-see-O-nah

The TV/phone/shower doesn't work.

**Favor de mostrarme cómo funciona esto.**
fah-BOR theh mos-TRAHR-meh KO-mo foon-see-O-nah EHS-to

Please show me how this works.

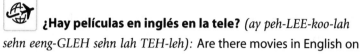 **¿Hay películas en inglés en la tele?** *(ay peh-LEE-koo-lah sehn eeng-GLEH sehn lah TEH-leh):* Are there movies in English on the TV?

Even in hotels in the United States or Canada, a misunderstanding on the final bill can spoil the mood when you check out. If you plan to use any television or Internet service, it is a good idea to know in advance what charges are involved. In luxury hotels some services may be included, just as in hotels north of the border.

| | |
|---|---|
| **¿Está incluido?** | Is it included? |
| ehs-TAH eeng-kloo-EE-thoh | |
| **¿Es gratis esto?** | Is this free? |
| ehs GRAH-tee SEHS-to | |

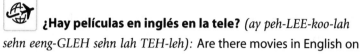 **¿Cobran por llamadas locales desde el cuarto?** *(KO-brahn por yah MAH-thahs lo-KAH-lehs dehs-dehl KWAHR-to):* Do you charge for local calls placed from the room?

Because you may need to place a local call, and phone service in Mexico can be tricky or impossible using a U.S.-based cell phone, it is a good idea to know in advance what a local call might cost. International calls are also problematic. You might do better with e-mail or an online computer-to-computer system for calls, depending on the situation.

Ironically, since much of Mexico was completely undeveloped, as it does develop communications in many areas, it is installing the latest technologies. Internet cafés, Wi-Fi, and other communications are quite common. Wherever Internet connections are available, they are often a better bet than trying to get a cell phone connection.

| | |
|---|---|
| **¿Hay acceso al Internet en mi cuarto?** | Is there Internet access in my room? |
| ay ahk-SEH-so ah leen-tehr-NEHT ehn mee KWAHR-to | |
| **¿Cuál es el código para conectarme?** | What is the code for getting connected? |
| KWAH leh sehl KO-thee-go PAH-ra ko-nek-TAHR-me | |

**Favor de despertarme a las... de la mañana/tarde/noche.**
*(fah-BOR deh dehs-pehr-TAHR-meh ah lahs... deh lah mahn-YAH-nah/TAHR-theh/NO-cheh):* Please wake me up at . . . in the morning/afternoon/night.

Some wake-up call systems are automated and bilingual, via touch-tone, but you may need to do it the old-fashioned way by talking to the front desk. You may need or want to explain why you want to get up when you do. The hotel personnel may tell you that you have more or less time than you think for making certain deadlines. Note that the English word *tour* is quite well-known in Mexican tourist areas.

| | |
|---|---|
| **El/La guía nos viene a buscar a las...** | The guide is coming for us at . . . |
| ehl/lah GHEE-ah nos bee-EH-neh ah boos-KAHR ah lahs | |
| **El vuelo sale a las...** | The flight leaves at . . . |
| ehl BWEH-lo SAH-leh ah lahs | |

**¿Cuáles son las horas de la alberca?** *(KWAH-leh son lah SO-rahs theh lahl BEHR-kah):* What are the pool hours?

If you are planning to enjoy the pool instead of the beach, you should know when to expect to find it open. It also helps to know what amenities are available poolside when planning your day.

In many thriving beach resorts, a number of entrepreneurial types have moveable stands on the beach itself or along the seaside avenue, called *el malecón* (ehl mah-leh-KOHN), where they sell or rent a wide variety of convenience foods, products, and services, from grilled foods to suntan lotion to beach umbrellas.

As is the case north of the border, swimming pools are for the exclusive use of the hotel guests and their friends. Still, these rules are often "guidelines." You may discover, in smaller hotels especially, that local children—employees' children or the newly made friends of a child on vacation—may be frolicking in the water as well. Mexicans tend to dote on their children, so be ready to be indulgent as well, at least where normal kid behavior is concerned. Remember, Mexicans don't like party poopers, whom they call, among other more colorful names, *matafiestas* (MAH-tah-fee-EHS-tahs), literally, "party killers."

| | |
|---|---|
| **Necesito una(s)/bata(s)/chancletas.** | I need a/some robe(s)/sandals. |
| neh-seh-SEE-to OO-nah(s) BAH-tah(s)/chang-KLEH-tah(s) | |
| **Quisiera almorzar al lado de la alberca.** | I'd like to eat lunch poolside. |
| kee-see-EH-ra ahl-mor-SAH rah LAH-tho theh lah ahl-BEHR-ka | |

**¿Hay un restaurante/bar en el hotel?** *(AY yoon rrehs-tah-oo-RAHN-teh/bah reh nehl o-TEHL):* Is there a restaurant/bar in the hotel?

Large resort hotels certainly have bars and restaurants on the premises. As one goes down the economic scale in terms of accommodations, it becomes less obvious what is part of the hotel and what is one of the businesses that have accumulated around it. Smaller port cities or towns, such as Puerto Peñasco, have more rustic accommodations and generally cater to weekenders, mostly from Arizona in the case of this town, which has its own name among English speakers who frequent it: Rocky Point.

In such places all the usual accommodations can be found, but not necessarily concentrated in one complex. This is changing as more condominiums, time-share resorts, and the like are being built. The point is, one needs to be ready to cobble together one's own tour, so to speak, at least for now. It's good to know the lay of the land.

| | |
|---|---|
| **¿Es este bar/restaurante parte del hotel?** | Is this bar/restaurant part of the hotel? |
| eh-SEHS-teh bahr/rehs-tah-oo-RAHN-teh PAHR-teh dehl o-TEHL | |
| **Quiero cargarlo a mi cuenta.** | I'd like to put this on my room tab. |
| kee-EH-ro kahr-GAHR-lo ah mee KWEHN-tah | |
| **¿Cuál es el mejor restaurante para mariscos?** | What is the best seafood restaurant? |
| KWAH leh sehl meh-HOR rehs-tah-oo-RAHN-teh PAH-ra mah-REES-kos | |

**Quisiera ver la cuenta, por favor.** *(kee-see-EH-ra behr lah KWEHN-tah por fah-BOR):* I'd like to see my bill, please.

In luxury resorts, as in the United States, checkout procedures are almost all automated and your bill appears under your door the morning of the day on which you are scheduled to leave. Of course, mistakes still can happen. You may not understand how something got on your bill, or you may wish to pay in some way other than with the same card with which you made your reservation.

If you see an error, or sense that there is one, remember that Mexicans find personal confrontations quite distasteful. Restrain your anger and try to focus on the error, not on how it happened. Above all, avoid any hint of personal blame regarding what may be merely a clerical error.

Once you're ready to leave and have resolved any issues, no matter how small, it is important to leave a good impression. Saying "Thanks for everything" (*Gracias por todo,* GRAH-see-ahs por TO-thoh) or "We really liked the hotel" (*Nos gustó mucho el hotel,* nos goos-TO MOO-cho eh lo-TEHL) are great things to say.

| | |
|---|---|
| **Creo que hay un error aquí.** | I think there's a mistake here. |
| KREH-o keh ay yoo neh-ROHR ah-KEE | |
| **Voy a pagar en efectivo/con esta** | I'll pay in cash/with this card. |
| **tarjeta.** | |
| BO-yah pah-GAHR eh neh-fehk- | |
| TEE-bo/ko nehs-tah tahr-HEH-tah | |

61

# Chapter 8

# Eating Out

**Quisiera ver el menú, por favor.** *(kee-see-EH-ra behr ehl meh-NOO por fah-BOR):* I'd like to see the menu, please.

Getting service in a restaurant is aided a bit by the fact that one has a menu to point to, and the selections in many sections are either intuitive or the words similar enough to English to make some educated guesses rather easy.

Just as a shopkeeper will ask "May I help you?" (*¿En qué puedo servirle?* ehn KEH PWEH-thoh sehr-BEER-leh), a waiter will invariably ask you "What may I offer you?" (*¿Qué se le ofrece?* keh seh leh o-FREH-seh). Your possible responses are either to tell the server what you want (if you already know), ask for a menu, or get a recommendation.

Most first-time travelers in Mexico are a bit surprised to learn that Mexican cuisine is quite varied, rich, and most important, very different from what they may have been exposed to in chain restaurants in the United States. The main meal for most Mexicans is lunch, served a bit later than its northern counterpart, after which one often senses that the pace of life slows for an hour or two and then resumes a quicker pace, even though there is no official *siesta* time. *Chilaquiles,* a popular breakfast item sure to appear on most menus, are best described as a sort of casserole in which yesterday's tortillas are put to use, along with eggs and, often, sausages. It has a more sophisticated cousin in the *tortilla española*, which is not a tortilla, or even an omelet as understood by this name in the United States, but a sort of Spanish quiche, often made with potatoes, olives, eggs, olive oil, and anchovies.

| | |
|---|---|
| **¿Qué tienen para desayunar/ almorzar/cenar?** | What do you have for breakfast/ lunch/dinner? |
| KEH tee-EH-nehn PAH-rah deh-sah- yoo-NAHR/ahl-mor-SAHR/ seh-NAHR | |
| **¿Podría traerme un plato de fruta?** | Could you bring me a fruit plate? |
| po-DREE-ah trah-EHR-meh oon PLAH-to theh FROO-tah | |

 **¿Cuál es el plato del día?** *(KWAH leh sehl PLAH-to thehl THEE-ah):* What is the special today?

Many restaurants, especially the smaller independent ones, will offer a daily special. Sometimes this is their pride and joy; other times it is simply a way of clearing inventory. If you really have no idea what you would like to try, asking for the menu is naturally the best bet. A dictionary can help you recognize the ingredients that may be mentioned on some menu items. To try to distinguish between a daily special and the house specialty, something in which they have some pride of ownership, you need to refine your question a bit.

**¿Cuál es la especialidad de la casa?**
KWAH-lehs lah ehs-peh-see-ah-lee-THAH theh lah KAH-sah

What is the house specialty?

**¿Qué me recomienda usted?**
KEH meh rreh-ko-mee-EHN-dah oos-TEHD

What do you recommend?

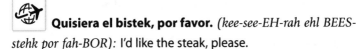 **Quisiera el bistek, por favor.** *(kee-see-EH-rah ehl BEES-stehk por fah-BOR):* I'd like the steak, please.

Just as many people in the United States are "meat and potatoes" eaters, many Mexicans, particularly in the northern and central regions, are "meat and beans" or "meat and tortilla" eaters, with rice taking some preference over potatoes for other starches. On the coasts, seafood abounds and rice and tortillas seem to be somewhat preferred over potatoes. Everywhere, chicken and pork will be featured in many local dishes as well.

For a real culinary adventure that may just rock your palate and transform your own kitchen when you return, you simply *must* try *mole* (MO-leh), a sauce typically made with raw cacao—unsweetened chocolate—and chilies. It seems that everyone's mother has her own recipe, so you are not likely to become bored if you explore this delightful and ample aspect of indigenous cuisines and do so in more than one restaurant.

**Prefiero el pollo asado.**
preh-fee-EH-ro ehl PO-yo ah-SAH-tho

I prefer the roasted chicken.

**¿Es muy picante?**
ehs MOO-ee pee-KAHN-teh

Is it very spicy?

**Quiero la carne a término medio.** *(kee-EH-ro lah KAHR-neh a TEHR-mee-no MEH-thee-o):* I'd like my meat cooked medium.

Unless you like your meat medium rare or rare, you should ask for this healthy and readily understood degree of doneness. If you order any meat other than fish, chicken, or pork, you'll be asked how you want it cooked: *¿A qué término?* (ah KEH TEHR-mee-no). If you make no selection, you will likely get medium to well done anyway. Other options are rare (*poco cocido,* PO-ko ko-SEE-thoh) and well done (*bien cocido,* bee-EHN ko-SEE-thoh).

Did you know that corn is native to the Americas? In Mexico there are many ways to enjoy it; one favorite is grilled corn on the cob, or *elote* (eh-LO-teh). There are a number of ingredients that the world owes to Mexico, first because of the biodiversity encountered by the natives and second because of their own agricultural and engineering ingenuity in cultivating them: chocolate, peanuts, tomatoes, and corn, to name a few. Besides the products themselves, there are cooking methods that we may think of as our own—barbecue, for instance. The English word is a corruption, or somewhat butchered pronunciation, of the Spanish phrase *de barba a cola*—literally "from chin to tail"—which is how Cortés described to the Emperor Charles V the way in which the Mexicans on the gulf coast cooked wild boars and tapirs—cousins of the pig: slow cooked whole, in a pit, smothered in a tomato-based sauce spiked with chilies . . . the original BBQ!

**Con papas/arroz, por favor.**       With potatoes/rice, please.
kon PAH-pahs/ah-RROS por fah-BOR
**¡Lo quiero tal y como lo comen**       I want it the way *you* eat it!
   **ustedes!**
loh kee-EH-ro tah lee KO-mo lo
   KO-mehn oos-TEH-thehs

¿**Es carne de res/de cerdo/cordero?** *(ehs KAHR-neh theh rehs/theh SEHR-thoh/kor-DEH-ro):* Is it beef/pork/lamb?

If the menu or the waiter says *carne*, you may want to clarify what sort of meat is meant. If it is chicken or fish, it will be more clearly stated. In other words, *carne* could mean beef, lamb, or pork. Some interesting local favorites may involve new or unusual ways of preparing familiar foods.

Mexican foods and styles of preparation vary greatly by region, as they do in Italy. Although nowadays most ingredients from anywhere can be had anywhere, regional tastes—demand combined with local pride—limit or determine just how much variety you might find in a given area. One example of *southern* Mexican cuisine is that of meat prepared in a pit, *al pibil* (ahl pee-BEEL), a method comparable to the Polynesian *imu*, a covered, slow-cooking fire pit fueled by heated volcanic stones. In the *pibil* style of cooking, some meats, particularly chicken stuffed with rice and herbs, are actually covered in moist clay before being placed in the pit, a method which helps retain the moisture and concentrate the flavors of the spices and herbs. The varieties are almost endless, so be adventurous.

The further south you go in Mexico, the less predictable and more varied the ingredients and styles of cooking will be. This is to be expected, since much of the cooking in the southwestern United States is similar, if not identical, to the food prepared a few steps away in Mexico. You will not be disappointed if you seek out restaurants in large cities that specialize in pre-Columbian cuisine—a source of culinary pride championed by Frida Kahlo, who collected and perfected many traditional dishes. A ceremonial shot of fine tequila is often the final touch on an evening of dining and is believed to aid in digestion.

| | |
|---|---|
| **¿Qué platos de pescado o mariscos tienen?** | What sort of fish or seafood dishes do you have? |
| keh PLAH-tos theh pehs-KAH-tho mah-REES-kos tee-EH-nehn | |
| **Tenemos una gran variedad de pescados y mariscos.** | We have a great variety of fish and seafood. |
| teh-NEH-mo soo-nah grahn bah-ree-eh-THAD theh pehs-KAH-tho ee mah-REES-kos | |
| **¿Tienen pollo al pibil?** | Do you have pit-roasted chicken? |
| tee-EH-nehn PO-yo ahl pee-BEEL | |

**¿Es a la parrilla/al carbón?** *(EH sah lah pah-REE-yah/ahl kahr-BON)*: Is it grilled?

Grilling, or cooking over the coals, is very popular everywhere in Mexico. You'll find that many vegetables are also grilled. One favorite that is becoming better known in northern climes is *nopales* (no-PAH-lehs), either pickled—*en conserva* (ehn kon-SEHR-bah) or grilled—*a la parrilla* (ah lah pah-REE-yah). The *nopal* (no-PAHL) is a cactus that may be seen on the emblem of Mexico, on the "tails" side of Mexican coins.

After being denuded of their thorns with a pair of tweezers or small pliers, or simply grilled to burn off the small, splinter-like thorns, *nopales* leaves are often sliced into slivers. They resemble green beans in appearance and even somewhat in flavor, but with a slightly citric taste and a bit of the viscosity of aloe. They are delicious and versatile. They are often used as another ingredient, like grilled onions or peppers, to fill a taco—not the hard, crusty things you find boxed up in U.S. supermarkets, but deliciously warm and soft corn or wheat flour tortillas heated on a grill.

**Por favor, tráigame los nopales**　　Please bring me the sliced *nopales*.
**rajados.**
por fah-BOR TRAH-ee-gah-me los
　　no-PAH-les rrah-HAH-thos
**No/me gustan las cebollas/**　　I do/don't like onions/chilies.
**los chiles.**
no/meh GOOS-tahn lahs seh-BO-
　　yahs/los CHEE-lehs

　　**Y para tomar, una cerveza.** *(ee PAH-rah to-MAH roo-nah sehr-BEH-sah):* And to drink, a beer.

Because of the tropical heat and fruits (and alcoholic beverages!), Mexico abounds in liquid refreshment. Although many guidebooks will tell you that *agua mineral* (AH-gwah mee-neh-RAHL) or *agua con gas* (AH-gwah kon GAHS) will get you sparkling water, I have found that naming the two major brands is most quickly understood by waiters.

The names of drinking vessels in Spanish are specific to the types of liquids served in them. Thus *una copa* (OO-nah KO-pah) is for wine, *una taza* (OO-na TAH-sah) is for hot drinks, and *un vaso* (oom BAH-so) is for water, milk, and juices.

**Quisiera Topo Chico/Peñafiel.**　　I'd like a Topo Chico/Peñafiel.
kee-see-EH-rah TO-po CHEE-ko/
　　PEHN-yah fee-EHL.
**Una taza de café negro/con**　　A cup of coffee/with milk and sugar.
**leche y azúcar.**
OO-nah TAH-sah theh kah-FEH NEH-
　　gro/kon LEH-che ee ah-SOO-kahr

**¿Tienen Uds. una lista de vinos?** *(tee-EH-nehn oos-TEH-thehs oo-nah LEES-tah theh BEE-nos):* Do you have a wine list?

Due to her hot climate and limited high elevations suitable for large-scale grape cultivation, Mexico cannot compete with U.S. producers, not to mention Chilean and Argentine growers, and is not known for wines. Notable exceptions exist, to be sure, coming from vineyards in Baja California Norte (just south of the California border) as well as from vineyards in the Sierras (Oriental and Occidental).

Interestingly, the word for *red* when speaking of wine is not *rojo*. So to ask for red wine, you must inquire about *vino tinto* (VEE-no TEEN-to). White wine is called *vino blanco* (VEE-no BLAHNG-ko), as one might expect.

Even though Mexico is producing wines that are good with European items on menus, the traditional drinks served with native Mexican foods still are the old standbys: beer, liqueurs for after-dinner drinks, and tequila for either mixed drinks or straight, as a one-shot ceremonial drink at the end of a meal. Mexican beers come in a variety that beer lovers will recognize: dark beers, such as Dos Equis or Negra Modelo and lighter, pilsner-style beers like Corona, Pacífico, and so forth.

**¿Me puede recomendar un buen vino mexicano?**
meh PWEH-theh rreh-ko-mehn-DAH room bwehn BEEno meh-hee-KAH-no

Can you recommend a good Mexican wine?

**Prefiero los vinos tintos/blancos.**
preh-fee-EH-ro los BEE-nos TEEN-tos/BLAHNG-kos

I prefer red/white wine.

**¿Tienen platos vegetarianos?** *(tee-EH-nehn PLAH-tos beh-heh-tah-ree-AH-nos)*: Do you have vegetarian dishes?

If you have special dietary concerns or committed preferences, it is good to know how to name them. Vegans, diabetics, and people with allergies are the most common. Saying you are allergic to something, even if not quite accurate, is often a diplomatic and effective way to avoid being served something you don't want or cannot eat.

Some travel websites that specialize in the dietary concerns of travelers have lists of restaurants and other details about shopping for specialty foods when traveling. Even a quick Internet search for *"restaurantes vegetarianos en México"* will yield numerous links. Some people may be surprised to realize that *yes*, there are vegetarians in Mexico.

| | |
|---|---|
| **Soy/es diabético/a.** | I am/He/She is diabetic. |
| soy/ehs dee-ah-BEH-tee-ko/ah | |
| **Yo no como carne.** | I do not eat meat. |
| yo no KO-mo KAHR-neh | |

**Y, de postre, quiero flan.** *(ee theh POS-treh kee-EH-ro flahn)*: And, for dessert, I'll have the flan.

On many Mexican menus, you'll discover that they have adopted the English word *pie*, but they have changed the spelling to *pay*, which, when pronounced according to the rules of Spanish, sounds almost exactly the same as our English pronunciation of the word *pie*. Somehow, the Spanish word *torta* didn't take hold as strongly, but you'll probably encounter it as well. Probably the proximity to the United States and exposure to our recipes for fruit pies tipped the linguistic balance northward.

Mexicans learned baking from the Spanish, and there is a plethora of fattening and luscious desserts to be sampled. But, that said, don't forget for a minute that Mexico is the mother country of chocolate. If you are a chocolate lover, you will return a worshipper of this substance, once taken for a god known by the name Xocolatl.

Most people think of Switzerland when they think of chocolate, or they recall some famous brand in some other country. Forget them all! There simply is no other place on earth that knows chocolate like Mexico, yet they seem to take it all in stride. Chocolate, and all it can do with other ingredients, such as its use with chilies to make *mole,* mentioned earlier, deserves the repeated, if not systematic, attention of any traveler with culinary intentions.

If you are serious about chocolate served the traditional Aztec way, you should make inquiries about where to find it. Unless you find specialists, unfortunately, you will sometimes be served . . . canned syrup. By searching *chocolate azteca* or *chocolate tradicional* you can find many wholesalers as well as restaurants in Mexico City and in large U.S. cities that specialize in pre-Columbian recipes using cacao.

**Busco restaurantes de cocina precolombina.**
I'm looking for restaurants with pre-Columbian cuisine.
BOOS-ko rrehs-tah-oo-RAHN-tehs theh ko-SEE-nah preh-ko-lom-BEE-na

**¿Tienen pastel de queso?**
Do you have cheesecake?
tee-EH-nehn pahs-TEHL theh KEH-so

# Chapter 9

# Entertainment

**Quisiera ver el baile folklórico.** *(kee-see-EH-rah beh rehl BAH-ee-leh fo-KLO-ree-ko):* I'd like to see the folk dance show.

Country music in the United States is often indebted to Mexican music, such as the use of the steel guitar. In fact, the steel guitar, familiar to most people for its contribution to Hawaiian music, is really a technique known as *huapango* (hoo-wah-PANG-go), found in some music of northern Mexico! It was exported to Hawaii and popularized there in the 1870s when Mexican ranch workers went to work on cattle ranches on the Big Island of Hawaii.

*Ranchera* music is Mexico's own home-grown country music and deals with themes similar to those of the country music of the United States. *Mariachi* is simply a name that refers to a small band that can play a number of styles, from *ranchera* music to more mellow, romantic music. *Boleros* are the Latin world's version of crooner or torch-singer music—the contemporaries of Sinatra and the big bands, swing, and jazz of the 1920s to beyond the mid-twentieth century.

**¿Hay un lugar donde pueda oír        una banda de mariachis?**
AH-yoon loo-GAHR DON-deh
    PWEH-tha o-EER OO-nah BAHN-
    dah theh mah-ree-AH-chees

Is there a place where I can hear a mariachi band?

**¿Dónde puedo escuchar música        ranchera en vivo?**
DON-theh PWEH-tho ehs-koo-CHAHR
    MOO-see-ka rrahn-CHEH-rah
    ehn BEE-bo

Where can I hear live country music?

**¿Hay una discoteca en el hotel?** *(AH-yoo na dees-ko-TEH-ka eh neh lo-TEHL):* Is there a disco in the hotel?

Yes, there are still discos in Mexico—or at least the name hasn't changed, even if the music and décor may have changed. If you are nostalgic for the era of spinning mirrored balls and colored lights on the ceiling, illuminated dance floors and the sounds of the mid-1970s, you can still find it alive and well in many upscale discos. It could be that the tourist crowd is mostly boomers, who knows? But if you're a boomer, or just want to find out what your parents danced to and what the scene was like, Mexico has the clubs to show you. One likely reason that disco is alive and well in many clubs in the Latin world in general is because of the influence of *salsa* music on that era—in other words, it's seen as more of a hybrid than an import.

As for another popular sort of club, be cautious about any non-hotel establishments called *cantinas*. They *can* be, but are not necessarily, places you wouldn't write to Mom about. Women in particular should steer clear of them, unless they are located on the grounds of a good hotel. Usually, the exterior of such places will reveal the sort of entertainment offered.

| | |
|---|---|
| **¿Adónde va la gente joven para divertirse?** | Where do young people go for fun? |
| ah-THOHN-deh bah lah HEHN-teh HO-behn PAH-rah dee-behr-TEER-seh | |
| **Quiero ir a un club de baile/ club nocturno.** | I want to go to a dance club/ nightclub. |
| kee-EH-ro eer ah oong kloob theh BAH-ee-leh/kloob nok-TOOR-no | |

 **¿Se está celebrando una fiesta municipal?** *(seh ehs-TAH seh-leh-BRAN-do oo-nah fee-EHS-tah moo-nee-see-PAHL):* Is there a local festival going on now?

If you are in need of fresh ideas for entertainment and are seeking local color, local people are usually a good source of information. Many cities and towns have festivals in honor of patron saints, similar in some respects to county fairs or farmers' markets in the United States, but much more festive and carnival-like in spirit. If you happen to be in a town during such a celebration, you are in for an interesting time.

Many local festivals will ostensibly honor a patron saint—every town has one, in addition to the well-known patron saints that Catholics everywhere would know. By now, *la Virgen de Guadalupe* is probably close to being universally recognized. You may have noticed that sometimes Carlos Santana wears her image on his guitar strap or includes her image in many of his concerts.

Catholic on the outside, many local festivals also reveal evidence of syncretism, the blending of pre-Columbian customs with western Catholic traditions, in subtle or sometimes not so subtle ways.

No holiday shows what syncretism is better than *El Día de los Muertos,* the Day of the Dead, Mexico's version of Halloween. It is a blend of Baroque Spanish Catholic notions and images of death blended with the Aztecs' already particular taste for such iconography. There are numerous websites where you can explore this subject. One thing our Halloween and the Day of the Dead have in common, other than their place in the liturgical calendar and its outwardly Catholic roots, is candy. You'll find candy skulls, often beautifully decorated.

If you are in Mexico anytime, but during Halloween especially, plan a trip to see *las momias de Guanajuato,* the mummies of Guanajuato. They are real dead people, standing, sitting, etc. inside a church, who were buried long enough for the local minerals to mummify them. Many of them have been standing reverently in a museum near the church for a long, long time, as their clothing will attest.

**¿Cuánto cuestan estas calaveras?**　　How much are these skulls?
KWAHN-to KWEHS-tahn EHS-tahs
　　kah-lah-BEH-rahs

**¿Hay alguna atracción turística**　　Is there a tourist attraction
　　**para niños?**　　　　　　　　　　for children?
AH yahl-GOO-nah ah-trak-see-ON
　　too-REES-tee-kah PAH-ra
　　NEEN-yos

**¿Adónde van las familias locales para divertirse?**
*(ah THON-deh BAHN lahs fah-MEE-lee-ahs lo-KAH-lehs PAH-rah dee-behr-TEER-seh)*: Where do local families go for fun?

If you want to get away from the tourist and disco scenes—particularly important if you are traveling as a family with children—find out what, if anything, the local families do. Be ready with a map so your informant can show you the way.

If that is not your wish, and you are seeking an almost homelike flavor, it won't surprise you to learn that nowadays large U.S.-style indoor shopping malls are as popular in Mexico as they are in the United States, especially in the hotter months.

Many of these indoor malls, such as Gran Plaza in Guadalajara, have food courts, restaurants, movie theaters, everything you might find in a U.S. mall, but you'll discover that the products, sounds, sights—and flavors—are different.

| | |
|---|---|
| **¿Hay una plaza comercial cerca?** | Is there a mall nearby? |
| ah-YOO-nah PLAH-sah ko-mehr-see-AHL SEHR-kah | |
| **¿Qué diversiones hay para adolescentes?** | What kinds of activities are there for teens? |
| keh dee-behr-see-O-nehs ay PAH-ra ah-thoh-leh-SEHN-tehs | |

**¿Hay cines con películas en inglés?** *(ay SEE-nehs kon peh-LEE-koo-lah seh neeng-GLEHS):* Are there movie theaters with movies in English?

Most, if not all, Hollywood productions can be found in larger cities. Movies made for small children, such as Disney classics, all are dubbed because the children are too young to read subtitles. If you are traveling with small children who like movies, be sure to take a few DVDs from home.

Most movies rated PG-13 and above have subtitles in Spanish. Going to the movies can offer an additional form of entertainment and education because you get to see and hear them in English as well as see what is funny or not to the Mexican audience and, judging by the reactions, who can understand the English.

**¿Qué películas dan ahora?**      What movies are they showing now?
keh peh-LEE-koo-lahs dah nah-O-rah
**¿Es doblada o tiene subtítulos?**      Is it dubbed or does it have subtitles?
ehs do-BLAH-thah o tee-EH-neh
   soob-TEE-too-los

 **¿Hay parques de diversiones para niños?** *(ay PAHR-kehs theh dee-behr-see-O-nehs PAH-rah NEEN-yos):* Are there amusement parks for kids?

If you have children who need to blow off steam, or if you want to tire them out so you can have some peace and quiet at night, you might inquire about amusement parks. Mexicans are very family-oriented and it is likely that there is something nearby, even if not quite an amusement park. Toy stores are also popular, in case you forgot to pack some or if you'd like to brighten your child's day.

A side trip from the usual tourist spectacles to see *artesanía mexicana* (ahr-teh-sah-NEE-ah meh-hee-KAH-nah) is always worthwhile. Many Mexican artisans make interesting and useful products and amusing toys—and not just for children. Their products include such things as marionettes and puppets, puzzles, games, and other ingenious objects. I am always intrigued by the varieties of chess sets, many carved from semiprecious stones. There are often whole neighborhoods or districts of cities where many artisans live and work. Their products are often made on a large scale and sold in export markets, such as a type of leather furniture called *equipales* (eh-kee-PAH-lehs) and tiles for kitchens, patios, and so forth. If you are in the area of Ciudad Juárez across from El Paso, take a trip to Pronaf Zone, where you can find a large number of handicraft items.

**Quiero ver artesanía mexicana.**   I'd like to see Mexican handicrafts.
kee-EH-ro behr ahr-teh-sah-NEE-ah
   meh-hee-KAH-nah
**Busco una tienda de juguetes.**   I'm looking for a toy store.
BOOS-ko OO-nah tee-EHN-dah
   theh hoo-GEH-tehs

**¿Hay un parque nacional para hacer caminatas cerca de aquí?** *(ay yoom PAHR-keh nah-see-o-NAHL PAH-rah sehr kah-mee-NAH-tahs SEHR-kah theh ah-KEE):* Is there a national park nearby where I could go hiking?

If your tastes, energies, and interests are in the outdoors, in walking, and sightseeing, you now have two questions to get you started and one pattern of response with some vocabulary.

Ecotourism is on the rise in Mexico, as is organic farming. Just notice how many more organic products at your local organic grocer's are coming with labels from Mexico. One type of excursion that you can't find in the United States is a tour of an agave field or tequila distillery. (The agave is the variety of cactus from which tequila is made.) Jalisco is the place to go for that! Of course, if you buy there, you'll get a slight discount compared to buying retail in a liquor store in Guadalajara, the capital of the state of Jalisco.

When you are off the beaten path in Mexico and think there could be nothing of cultural or historical interest, you are almost always mistaken. Mexico's long, reasonably well researched pre-Columbian past means that most places have some bragging rights. Most cities of moderate size boast some kind of museum housing art or objects from the colonial period or from the period of the Mexican Revolution, which happened a mere four generations ago (1911). In Ciudad Juárez I recall seeing the actual car in which Pancho Villa was riding when he was assassinated, bullet holes and all, in a small museum not far from the main cathedral.

| | |
|---|---|
| **¿Hay excursiones para ver lugares de interés histórico?**<br>ah yehk-skoor-see-O-nehs PAH-rah behr loo-GAH-rehs theh een-teh-REH sees-TO-ree-ko | Are there tours to places of historic interest? |
| **¿Hay iglesias/catedrales/ museos aquí?**<br>ay yee-GLEH-see ahs/kah-teh-DRAH-lehs/moo-SEH-o sah-KEE | Are there churches/cathedrals/ museums here? |

**¿Cuál es la mejor excursión para una familia?** *(KWAH lehs lah meh-HOR eks-koor-see-ON PAH-ra OO-nah fah-MEE-lee-ah):* What is the best tour for families?

If you are traveling with a family or group consisting of people of different ages and interests, finding a tour or activity that offers everyone something might require a bit of research. Sometimes it just takes making special needs known.

Unlike in the United States, where the Americans with Disabilities Act lends a certain uniformity, Mexican infrastructure is varied and wheelchair access is often limited to the newest buildings and the more sophisticated forms of travel. Traveling with children is never easy, but traveling with a disabled person of any age can often be especially problematic, particularly where access is concerned.

**¿Hay excursiones para personas que usan una silla de ruedas?**
ay eks-koor-see-O-nehs PAH-rah pehr-SO-nahs keh OO-sahn OO-nah SEE-yah theh roo-EH-dahs

Are there tours for people in wheelchairs?

**¿Ofrecen una actividad turística para ancianos?**
o-FREH-seh NOO-nahk-tee-bee- THAHD too-REES-tee-kah PAH-rah ahn-see-AH-nos

Do you offer a tourist activity for elderly people?

# Chapter 10

# Museums

---

**¿Dónde está el Museo Nacional de Antropología?** *(DON-thehs TAH ehl moo-SEH-o nah-see-o-NAHL deh ahn-tro-po-lo-HEE-ah):* Where is the National Anthropology Museum?

---

Travelers to Mexico often underestimate the history of the country, partly because many of its current woes are too visible—crowding, pollution, and poverty, to name three that quickly meet the eye. Mexico was the country where the great Aztec Empire was as mighty as Rome and arguably richer in natural resources, biological and agricultural diversity, and even in terms of her population.

When Cortés landed in 1519, it is estimated that 15 million people lived within Mexico's modern borders. For some fascinating reading, I recommend obtaining a copy of Hernán Cortés's Second Letter to Charles V (sent in 1522), which is available in English online. His descriptions are stunning. Many of the places he mentions, such as the engineering wonder of Xochimilco, the floating gardens in Mexico City, are still there and still beautiful.

| | |
|---|---|
| **¿Hay excursiones organizadas para ver los museos?** | Are there organized tours for seeing the museums? |
| ay ehs-koor-see-O-nehs or-gah-nee-SAH-thas PAH-rah behr los moo-SEH-os | |
| **¿Se ofrecen excursiones para ver Xochimilco?** | Are there tours of Xochimilco? |
| seh o-FREH-sehn ehs-koor-see-O-nehs PAH-rah behr sho-chee-MEEL-ko | |

**¿Cuánto cuesta la entrada?** *(KWAHN-to KWEHS-tah lah ehn-TRAH-thah):* How much is the entrance fee?

If you love museums, Mexico, particularly Mexico City, has some of the finest in the world. Naturally, their greatest collections deal with pre-Columbian art and culture. Many of the artifacts are breathtaking and offer a glimpse into the world of our continent before the arrival of Europeans. You may have a particular type of museum in mind, such as a museum dealing with the Revolution or even of particular trades, such as railroads or mining.

Seeing the treasure troves of ancient America is worth the price of admission, and the museums of Mexico City in particular are the mother lode. Many will offer price structures for groups, students, the elderly, and kids. There likely will be a sign posted with the prices, but since you may not know enough Spanish to recognize it immediately, it never hurts to ask.

**¿Ofrecen descuentos para grupos/niños?**
o-FREH-sehn dehs-KWEHN-tos PAH-rah GROO-pos/NEEN-yos

Do you offer group/child discounts?

**¿Podemos salir y volver sin pagar de nuevo?**
po-THEH-mos sah-LEE-ree bol-BER seen teh-NEHR keh pah-GAHR deh NWEH-bo

Can we leave and come back without having to pay again?

**¿Cuáles son las horas del museo?** *(KWAH-leh son lah SO-rahs dehl moo-SEH-o):* What are the museum's hours?

Assuming you are in Mexico City and have a limited number of days and hours per day to see museums, it is a good idea to sit down and organize your tour unless you are part of a packaged tour. The advantage of going alone is, of course, flexibility, but you have the downside of having to work out your own schedule, which means gathering information. Personally, I find it pays to go it alone, since you can stay longer in one place if it catches your fancy or if you wish to shop or just browse in the gift shops longer than a package tour might allow.

On the other hand, going on a package tour means less stress about directions and ground transportation. If you have an extra day and want to revisit a museum you didn't get enough time to see on the tour, you can go back on your own and get the best of both strategies.

**¿Están abiertos todos los días de semana y los fines de semana?**
ehs-TAHN ah-bee-EHR-tos TO-thos los THEE-ahs de seh-MAH-nah ee los FEE-nehs theh seh-MAH-nah

Are you open weekdays and weekends?

**¿A qué hora se abre/se cierra el museo?**
ah keh O-rah seh see-EH-ra/seh AH-breh ehl moo-SEH-o

What time does the museum open/close?

 **¿Tienen ascensores?** *(tee-EH-nehn ah-sehn-SO-rehs)*: Do you have elevators?

For practical as well as safety reasons, you may need to ask how to get into and out of a building. In addition, you should ask about any special needs you can anticipate, such as wheelchair access, *before* paying. Older museums, more likely to be found in smaller cities and towns, may not yet be fitted with ramps.

**¿Dónde está la entrada/salida más cercana?**
DON-dehs TAH lah ehn-TRAH-tha/ sah-LEE-thah mah sehr-KAH-nah

Where is the nearest entrance/exit?

**¿Hay un restaurante o cafetería en el museo?**
ay yoon rrehs-tah-oo-RAHN-teh o kah-feh-teh-REE-ah eh nehl moo-SEH-o

Is there a restaurant or café in the museum?

**Busco la colección de la época colonial.** *(BOOS-ko lah ko-lek-see-ON deh lah EH-po-kah ko-lo-nee-AHL):* I'm looking for the colonial period collection.

Mexico's colonial period extends from shortly after the fall of Tenochtitlán (present-day Mexico City) to the Spanish in 1521 to the beginning of Mexico's War of Independence from Spain, September 16, 1810. Mexico's fight for independence was led at first by a priest, Father Miguel Hidalgo. No portraits of him were allowed by the Spanish government, so the image found on Mexican paper money is an idealized portrait gleaned from descriptions.

Sor Juana, a Mexican nun, was one of the most prolific writers of her time and one of the first modern defenders of women's right to learn and study. Her image, found on the 1,000 peso note, is from a famous portrait. One oil portrait of her is found in the Philadelphia Museum of Art and the other in the Museo Nacional de Antropología e Historia in Mexico City.

In post-colonial times, the art of José Guadalupe Posada, Diego Rivera, and many others is strongly indigenous in flavor and often reveals a strong collectivist and nativist spirit—the soul of Mexico's Revolution.

**¿Dónde está la colección de arte azteca/precolombina?**
DON-dehs-TAH lah ko-lek-see-ON de AHR-teh ahs-TEH-kah/preh-ko-lom-BEE-nah

Where is the Aztec/pre-Columbian collection?

**Me gustaría ver el retrato de Sor Juana.**
meh goos-tah-REE-ah beh rehl rreh-TRAH-to theh sor hoo-AH-na

I'd like to see the portrait of Sor Juana.

87

**¿Tienen un tour en inglés?** *(tee-EH-neh noon too reh neeng-GLEHS):* Do you have a tour in English?

As in the United States, many large museums provide recorded tours in various languages on individual headsets. If they do not have that technology, they still may have a docent who can do tours in English. In most museums, even some of the most modest, there will be a brochure in English even if they have no English-speaking docent or taped tour.

The good thing about museums is that often the objects speak for themselves. If you find yourself or your group linguistically isolated, take heart! There is an educational opportunity in having to observe closely and see if you can figure out why a particular object is there—in a way, everyone gets to be an archaeologist. This is a good strategy to use with children, since they respond to a more socially interactive mode of learning.

| | |
|---|---|
| **¿Hay un tour en casete?** | Is there a recorded tour? |
| ay YOON toor ehn kah-SEH-teh | |
| **Mis audífonos no funcionan.** | My headphones don't work. |
| mee sah-oo-DEE-fo-nos no foon-see-O-nahn | |

**¿Hay alguna exhibición especial ahora?** *(ay YAHL-goo-nah eks-see-bee-see-ON ehs-peh-see-AH lah-O-rah):* Is/Are there any special exhibit/s now?

If there is a traveling exhibition, particularly of pre-Columbian art, it is probably spectacular and worth seeing. Some exhibits from South America, from Inca or Moche cultures, will occasionally make the rounds, staying for a while in other great museums and then moving on.

Just as the King Tut exhibit that once toured the museums of the world, they aren't likely to return. The moral of the story is that if you have a love of antiquities and happen to be in town when something special is on display, it is a chance of a lifetime you should not miss.

| | |
|---|---|
| **¿Hasta cuándo va a estar esta exhibición?** | How long will this exhibit be here? |
| AHS-tah KWAHN-do bahs TAHR ehs-tah ehk-see-bee-see-ON | |
| **¿Tienen un tour para niños?** | Do you have a children's tour? |
| tee-EH-neh noon toor PAH-rah NEEN-yos | |

**¿Dónde está la tienda de regalos?** *(DON-dehs-TAH lah tee-EHN-dah theh rreh-GAH-los):* Where is the gift shop?

If you spend a great deal of time and effort to go to Mexico and see her treasures, it is a good idea to bring back something other than photos or memories. You probably will want to pick up mementos or items to send to friends. If you are a teacher, you may want to take home some educational materials.

In Mexico the word *timbre* (TEEM-breh), which also means doorbell, is the most common word for a postage stamp. Envelopes are probably not sold separately in museum shops, but if you need to inquire, they are *sobres* (SO-brehs).

| | |
|---|---|
| **¿Tienen un libro sobre la colección de...?** | Do you have a book about the . . . collection? |
| tee-EH-neh noon LEE-bro SO-breh lah ko-lek-see-ON deh | |
| **Quisiera comprar una reproducción de...** | I'd like to buy a copy of . . . |
| kee-see-EH-ra kom-PRAH roo-nah rreh-pro-dook-see-ON deh | |

**Me gustaría comprar aretes con un diseño azteca.** *(meh goos-tah-REE-ah kom-PRAH rah-REH-tehs ko noon dee-SEHN-yo ahs-TEH-kah):* I'd like to buy earrings with an Aztec design.

Shopping in a museum gift shop does not require the bartering skills necessary for survival in a *tianguis,* or open-air native market. It is likely that the items for sale will be reproductions of many of the items on display. Oftentimes, the jewelry items will be of silver—one of Mexico's most plentiful precious metals.

The silver mined from Taxco comes out of the ground quite pure, as much as 90 percent in some cases. Silver jewelry made from Taxcan silver is stamped with the word Taxco in some inconspicuous place, such as the inside of a ring. Other commonly used materials include turquoise (*turquesa* toor-KEH-sah), lapis lazuli (*lapis lázuli* lah-pees LAH-soo-lee), onyx (*ónix* O-neeks), jade (*jade* HA-theh), and obsidian (*obsidiana* ob-see-thee-AH-nah).

| | |
|---|---|
| **¿Tienen pulseras/sortijas/ broches?** | Do you have bracelets/rings/ brooches? |
| tee-EH-nehn pool-SEH-rahs/ sor-TEE-hahs/BRO-chehs | |

**¿Hay un lugar seguro donde pueda dejar la mochila?** *(ah yoon loo-GAHR seh-GOO-ro DON-deh PWEH-tha deh-HAHR lah mo-CHEE-lah):* Is there a safe place where I can leave my backpack?

Check it in or risk losing it, and if you find something, try to get it to the rightful owner by taking it to the check-in area. It is a good idea to master the essential vocabulary for dealing with lost-and-found situations. The handy little word for *this*, *esto* (EHS-to), will enable you to save time by avoiding having to look up the name of the thing you have found or wish to check in.

| | |
|---|---|
| **He perdido mi bolsa/billetera/ sombrero.** | I have lost my purse/wallet/hat. |
| eh pehr-DEE-tho mee BOL-sah/ bee-yeh-TEH-ra/som-BREH-ro | |
| **Alguien ha perdido esto.** | Someone has lost this. |
| AHL-ghee-eh nah pehr-DEE-tho EHS-to | |

# Chapter 11

# Common Warning Signs

Most, if not all, of the phrases elsewhere in this phrasebook are things that you might say. The items included in this section are far less often said than they are posted as silent sentinels meant to keep you safe. The variety of ways in which signage in Mexico is made and displayed is worthy of serious sociological study and reveals what a multi-modal society Mexico is. Octavio Paz, one of Mexico's great intellectuals of the twentieth century, referred to Mexico as a pyramidal society, one in which some of its citizens are living in penthouses as grand as any in Manhattan, while others live in a nineteenth-century rural environ-ment, and still others in a medieval world. There are many convents and monasteries that have been in continuous existence for centuries. At the other extreme, there are still many Mexicans, particularly in the Yucatán peninsula, whose daily lives are little impacted by the arrival of Europeans.

Likewise, signage may be as sophisticatedly made and posted as any in Switzerland. It may also be made at a local print shop with good materials, but with misspellings. A construction worker might hastily scrawl a warning sign to pedestrians, using his carpenter's pencil on a piece of dirty cardboard. You get the idea! The lack of standardiza-tion may make newcomers feel as if they have to read everything just to keep on their toes. But really, if you are aware of your surroundings and realize that you do need to be more vigilant simply because you are in an unfamiliar environment, you'll do fine.

 **Aviso** *(ah-BEE-so)*: Warning

The most common warning sign says just that, as a heading. It is as likely to be found on a door as on a package insert for an over-the-counter drug. It does not mean only *warning,* however. It can also mean *notice,* as in public notice. Nowadays, when the message below has to do with safety, the sign is usually more specific and will be more standardized than not. It also will likely include graphics to show what the danger is, if that is its meaning. The following phrase always refers to some sort of risk.

**Precaución**                              Warning
preh-kah-oo-see-ON

 **Peligro** *(peh-LEE-gro)*: Danger

When you see this sign, do pay attention, no matter how unsophisticated the sign. It could be that a construction foreman put it up before leaving a work site because he discovered exposed wiring near the sidewalk his crew was breaking up and, having no sign at hand, grabbed a magic marker and a piece of plywood so he could warn pedestrians. A "real" sign may or may not appear after that.

After one of Guadalajara's famous summer storms, I recall seeing downed electrical wires for two weeks near the university. No sign was ever posted. I suppose if you see downed wires, you should have the sense to avoid them—and young children can't read anyway.

| | |
|---|---|
| **Peligro de descarga** | Danger of shock |
| peh-LEE-gro theh dehs-KAHR-gah | |
| **Peligro de muerte** | Danger of death |
| peh-LEE-gro theh MWER-teh | |

**No fumar** *(no foo-MAHR):* No smoking

Many Mexicans smoke. In fact, the popularity of smoking resembles the popularity of prophets, who are more popular in other countries than at home. You are more likely to see this sign in restaurants and hotels that cater to a lot of upscale locals and tourists.

You are not likely to see it in other establishments other than airplanes—and then watch out when you leave U.S. airspace. If you want a non-smoking seat, make very clear that you don't want to be near the area where smoking might still be allowed. Notices asking the public not to sit in certain seats or areas may be found on planes and in restaurants, concert halls, and other public venues.

| | |
|---|---|
| **No se permite fumar** | Smoking prohibited |
| no seh pehr-MEE-teh foo-MAHR | |
| **No sentarse** | Do not sit here |
| no sehn-TAHR-seh | |

**Prohibida la entrada** *(pro-ee-BEE-tha lahn TRAH-thah):* No entrance

This is a sign found on highways or on doors. In the first case, it is meant to prevent head-on collisions; in the second, to restrict areas to service staff or employees. The next entry, beginning with the same words, is found on the entrances to the types of nocturnal entertainment one does not take families to. Minors, officially known as *menores de edad* (meh-NO-rehs theh eh-THAD), are excluded for obvious reasons. Women are excluded too. Perhaps this is due to the remnants of neo-Victorian morality one still encounters in Mexico, or perhaps it's a manifestation of the double standard imposed by benevolent machismo. Whatever the reason, the sign is posted to protect women from having the reputation of the women who work there. The prohibition against uniformed personnel is more universally logical. It refers to people such as police officers and fire department employees who are on duty.

| | |
|---|---|
| **Prohibida la entrada de niños, mujeres y uniformados** | Minors, women and uniformed personnel not admitted |
| pro-ee-BEE-tha lahn TRAH-thah theh NEEN-yos moo-HEH-reh see oo-nee-for-MAH-thos | |

**Piso mojado** *(PEE-so mo-HAH-tho):* Wet floor

Spanish is now the unofficial second language of the United States. Regardless of your views on immigration, history, or national identity, it is likely to stay that way—and increasingly move into the public sphere, even if immigration were to stop tomorrow. Since so many people who work in the service and maintenance sectors are Spanish speakers, this sign has become almost as common in the United States as it is in Mexico.

The same may be said of the first phrase below as well, since many standard sign makers in the United States are printing them bilingually. The last phrase is also found on Internet sites under development, just as its English translation is.

| | |
|---|---|
| **Pintura fresca** | Fresh paint |
| peen-TOO-rah FREHS-kah | |
| **En obras** | Under construction |
| ehn O-brahs | |

 **No hay devolución** *(no ay theh-bo-loo-see-ON)*: No returns

This is a sign you are likely to see posted in a shop. Because it is not a phrase *you* would say, it appears here and not in the shopping section. Often it is accompanied by the words *sin comprobante* (seen com-pro-BAHN-teh), or *without receipt*. Even with a receipt, a shop owner is unlikely to be willing to lose the original sale, and so store credit is offered. If you are a tourist, this means finding another item in the store that you like.

**En caso de incendio...** *(ehn KAH-so theh een-SEHN-dee-o)*: In case of fire . . .

If posted on a glass case containing firefighting equipment, you'll know what to do. Unsurprisingly, firefighting signs are among the most standardized and up-to-date in the country, as is the equipment.

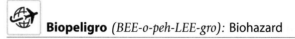 **Biopeligro** *(BEE-o-peh-LEE-gro):* Biohazard

By law, international agreement, and by the decrees and training of the various professionals involved in biologics, biohazard signs are supposed to be clearly marked with the biohazard symbol you see in restrooms and medical centers in the United States.

**Desechos biopeligrosos/químicos**   Biohazard/chemical waste
deh SEH-chos BEE-o-peh-lee-
  GRO-sos/KEE-mee-kos

 **Agua contaminada** *(AH-gwah kon-tah mee-NAH-thah):* Contaminated water

Given the already uneven water purity in Mexico, a sign like this is a sure indicator of a serious problem due to either chemicals or bacteria. It could be posted near a spigot, a stream, a lake, or even a beach (as I've seen near South Beach in San Diego on more occasions than I can count). If posted near a spigot, the water is likely to be unfiltered and untreated runoff for irrigation purposes.

**Agua no potable**                    Water not for/unsuitable for drinking
AH-goo-ah no po-TAH-bleh
**Aguas prietas**                      Dirty water
AH-goo-ahs pree-EH-tahs

 **Vibrador** *(bee-brah-DOR):* Speed bump/rumble strip

If you are traveling by car or bus, sooner or later you'll see this sign. Have a laugh if you want. It really does only mean *speed bump* or *rumble strip.* In other words, it doesn't bring a smile to the lips of Mexican drivers, but if you burst out laughing when you see it, you'll get puzzled looks from locals.

Here are some other common highway signs. The one about curves is often employed in the plural to refer to a femme fatale: *curvas peligrosas.*

**Despacio**                    Slow
dehs-PAH-see-o

**Curva peligrosa**             Dangerous curve
KOOR-bah peh-lee-GRO-sah

 **Guarde su distancia** *(GWAHR-deh soo dees-TAHN-see-ah):* Keep your distance/back off

This is a sign found on the rear of trucks carrying heavy or dangerous loads. If you see this sign on the back of a truck, it definitely means that what it carries is either in danger of tipping under adverse conditions or is dangerous in and of itself, such as chemicals or gasoline. On the other hand, if you don't see this sign on a large truck, it could *still* be carrying something you don't want to be near in a highway emergency.

This phrase might also be posted on doors to high-voltage utility closets or other enclosures (along with a warning about electrical shock). It could even be said by a police officer or other person engaged in serious crowd control.

# Chapter 12

# Health Issues

**Necesito ver a un médico.** *(neh-seh-SEE-to beh rah oon MEH-thee-ko):* I need to see a doctor.

The quality and availability of health care in Mexico varies more widely than in the United States or Canada. In large cities, you can find health care every bit as sophisticated as in the best hospitals north of the Río Grande. Given the complexities of coverage in the United States, in particular with HMOs, PPOs and so forth, it is important to find out from your provider how, or whether, you can be covered in the event of a medical emergency while you are away.

Many doctors and dentists in private practice in Mexico simply hang up their shingles and are paid directly by their patients without any insurer in the middle. For minor complaints or a filling that just can't wait, this is certainly convenient, although some find it unsettling.

In Mexico, and indeed in much of the rural southwestern United States, there is a spectrum of assimilation of modern Western medicine among Mexicans. At one extreme, one finds people who are fully on board with modern medicine. At the other, one finds people who will go only to shamans of various sorts whose practices are anthropologically interesting, and at times effective, due to some serious expertise in the use of native plants.

In between these extremes, you find people who are hedging their bets by combining the two extremes in different ways, much as many Americans will consult an expert in Chinese medicine or ayurvedic medicine as well as their HMO. Mexican shamanistic practices have their roots in pre-Columbian practices, combined with medieval Spanish medicine.

| | |
|---|---|
| **¿Hay una sala de urgencias cerca de aquí?** | Is there an emergency room nearby? |
| ay YOO-nah SAH-lah theh oor-HEN-see-ahs SEHR-ka theh ah-KEE | |
| **Necesitamos ver a un pediatra/ ginecólogo/dentista.** | We need to see a pediatrician/ gynecologist/dentist. |
| neh-seh-see-TAH-mos beh rah oon peh-thee-AH-trah/hee-neh-KO-lo-go/dehn-TEES-tah | |

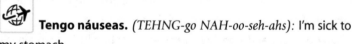 **Tengo náuseas.** *(TEHNG-go NAH-oo-seh-ahs):* I'm sick to my stomach.

OK, let's be honest: don't call it Moctezuma's revenge. Your doctor might, since everyone in Mexico is familiar with the term, but the truth is that if foreigners refer to the intestinal upsets caused by bacteria such as E-coli or salmonella as Moctezuma's revenge, some Mexicans feel offended. They take it as a comment on cleanliness. In many cases such infections do have to do with a lack of care and sanitation in handling food, but many Mexicans get similar upsets when they travel north; it's a matter of different sets of germs.

Managing minor cases of diarrhea can be as simple as going to the pharmacy or having someone bring you something. Cases that go on for more than a day or are severe should be looked after quickly. Some bugs are very strange indeed. I recall being sick for two weeks, but for only one hour at the same time each night, after which I was fine again and had an appetite and plenty of energy. Another time, I was living alone and a neighbor, an elderly woman with plenty of experience in home remedies, gave me *horchata* to drink. As its principal ingredient is rice, it did the trick within a few hours.

**Hace dos días que tengo diarrea.**    I've had diarrhea for two days.
AH-seh thos DEE-ahs keh TEHNG-go
   thee-ah-RREH-ah
**¿Será una intoxicación?**    Could it be food poisoning?
seh-RAH OO-nah een-tok-see-
   ka-see-ON

**Tengo un dolor de pecho.** *(TEHNG-go oon do-LOR theh PEH-cho):* I have a pain in my chest.

Describing symptoms can be frustrating, even in one's own language. Having to do so in another language can make you feel as if you may as well go to a veterinarian. After all, they are the only medical practitioners who don't ask their patients questions!

If you have any condition that you think could present a problem, it is a good idea to know the name of it in Spanish. Think of it as having a medical alert bracelet in verbal form. Since it is important to have a heartbeat, we begin there!

103

One fortunate thing about anatomical vocabulary is that in both English and Spanish, most of the terminology that goes beyond gross anatomy is Latin based. If you took biology in high school or college and can recall the formal names of organs, you'll have a head start if you need to talk to a doctor or dentist who knows no English.

**Creo que es el corazón.**          I think it's my heart.
KREH-o keh sehl ko-rah-SON
**Estoy mareado.**          I'm dizzy.
ehs-TOY mah-reh-AH-tho

**Estoy embarazada.** *(ehs-TOY yehm-bah-rah-SAH-thah):* I am pregnant.

If you travel by air to Mexico when you are pregnant, it is highly unlikely that you will be giving birth there, since airlines have policies that prohibit women from flying after a certain stage of pregnancy. Of course, if you are traveling by boat or car, and are farther along, you just might go into labor.

It is also more likely that you may find yourself in a rural area if you are traveling by car. Mexico's high birth rates do mean that even doctors in general private practice have had to deal with obstetrics. It's best not to travel at that time, so speak to your doctor before even thinking of traveling when you are pregnant.

My wife and I found out about her pregnancy after we arrived, and we had to stay for a few months. Fortunately, everything was fine. We were only there for the first trimester and we had a friend who was a physician.

**Me siento mal aquí.**                     It hurts here.

meh see-EHN-to mahl-ah-KEE

**Me duele la espalda.**                    My back hurts.

meh THWEH-leh lah ehs-PAHL-dah

**¿Se requiere una receta médica para esto?** *(seh rreh-kee-EH-reh oo-nah rreh-SEH-tah MEH-thee-kah PAH-rah EHS-to)*: Do I need a prescription for this?

If you or anyone you are traveling with needs regular medical attention, or needs to have prescriptions filled so often that it will be necessary to have one filled while in Mexico, it is advisable to make arrangements beforehand.

On the positive side, many medications can be purchased in Mexico without a prescription, and for much less. Pharmacists are licensed to do what we might call practicing medicine without a license, but they do have limits concerning what and how much they can prescribe. Along with ecotourism, medical tourism is becoming popular, but as with any medical course of action, beware of charlatans.

**¿Es costoso este medicamento?**          Is this medication expensive?

ehs-kos-TO-so EHS-teh meh-
    thee-ka-MEHN-to

**¿Se puede tomar esto con...?**           Can I take this with . . . ?

seh PWEH-theh to-MAH rehs-to kon

**¿Dónde está la farmacia más cercana?** *(DON-thehs TAH lah fahr-MAH-see-ah mahs sehr-KAH-nah):* Where is the nearest pharmacy?

Most drug companies provide package inserts in more than one language. If not, I have noticed that in large Mexican pharmacies there is often an English-language copy of the *Physicians' Desk Reference* or the *Merck Manual* in which you can read about the drug you have been prescribed if you are not already familiar with it.

Many people who live just north of the border go to Mexico, not just for cheaper gasoline, but also for cheaper drugs. Be careful with narcotic or opiate painkillers and products containing pseudoephedrine, since they are controlled substances. You don't want to have a lot of explaining to do when re-entering the United States or Canada.

**Necesito aspirina/algo para la tos.**   I need aspirin/something for a cough.
neh-seh-SEE-to ahs-pee-REE-nah/
   AHL-go PAH-ra lah TOS
**Soy alérgico a...**                      I'm allergic to . . .
soy ya-LEHR-hee-ko ah

**Me he torcido el tobillo.** *(meh eh tor-SEE-tho ehl to-BEE-yo):* I have twisted my ankle.

Whether you're a hiker or not, walking can still be risky in and of itself, even on city sidewalks. Uneven sidewalks are a common problem in Mexico, as are potholes in roads, uneven curbs, and other hazards. Besides watching a bit more where you are walking, you need to be ready to get help for the scrape or bruise that can result from tripping and falling.

People who have joint problems, or have been treated in some way for them, need to be able to communicate that bit of health history to a doctor if there is a possibility of having to perform an invasive procedure. If it can wait until you return, you're probably wise to do so—not so much because of any lack of expertise, but because of your need to communicate well with your health care provider and to follow up.

Pain can often be managed without prescriptions in Mexico, and crutches, a cane, and ice are not difficult to obtain if you sprain an ankle. Then there is always the possibility of self-medicating a minor mishap with a margarita.

| | |
|---|---|
| **Estoy sangrando.** | I'm bleeding. |
| ehs-TOY sahng-GRAHN-do | |
| **Me he hecho un esguince en** | I've sprained my back/arm/shoulder. |
| **la espalda/el brazo/el hombro.** | |
| meh eh EH-cho oo- nes-GEEN-ceh | |
| en lahs PAHL-dah/ehl BRAH-so/ | |
| ehl OM-bro | |

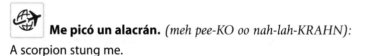 **Me picó un alacrán.** *(meh pee-KO oo nah-lah-KRAHN)*: A scorpion stung me.

Talking about broken bones, scrapes, and cuts is seldom necessary, since the wound can speak for itself to a doctor or nurse. But it can be very important to be able to describe a venomous creature that may have bitten or stung you.

Of all the creatures you are likely to encounter in Mexico that might cause you to need medical attention, the scorpion tops the list. Do not leave clothes in a pile. Do not reach into any area where leaves, sticks, or other rubbish may have lain undisturbed for even a few hours. An old wooden chest of drawers can often make an attractive home for scorpions.

Not all scorpions are created equal. Surprisingly, the smaller scorpions are often the most venomous. They all are creepy to look at. They are members of the arachnid family, like spiders. Unlike spiders, they do not jump, but they are good at climbing. If you are staying in a resort it is unlikely that you'll find scorpions in your room, but they can find a way in via luggage.

Call me paranoid, but before getting into bed, even in a nice place, I pull the sheets down all the way to the foot of the bed to see if I have an unwanted bedmate. Unless I am staying in a luxury hotel, I move the bed at least six inches away from the wall.

In all the years that I have pulled down the sheets, I've never found a scorpion. The one time I might forget though, could be the time I regret not having taken the precaution. I've never been stung either, although I have killed a few in bathtubs (they come up through the drains) and in hallways, defying me to pass. If you are stung by one, seek attention and be able to tell how big it was and what color.

| | |
|---|---|
| **Deme algo para el dolor.** | Give me something for the pain. |
| DEH-meh AHL-go PAH-rahl do-LOR | |
| **¿Tienen el antídoto?** | Do you have the antidote? |
| tee-EH-neh neh lahn-TEE-do-to | |

**Tengo seguro médico.** *(TEHNG-go seh-GOO-ro MEH-thee-ko):* I have medical insurance.

Paperwork is bad enough in English. Some of what you'll see on a form will be intuitive: a place for your name, address, and so forth. It is likely that payment will be expected at the time of treatment and you'll have to deal with your insurer when you return. As stated earlier, these are questions you should ask your carrier before you travel, just in case.

In the United States and Canada forms are often available in multiple languages. In Mexico, however, you may not find an English version of the form you might be asked to fill out. The reason is simple and has nothing to do with anti-foreign sentiment, as some people have suggested, seeking to point out that we are somehow too tolerant and indulgent with foreigners, while they are not. Mexico does not have large immigrant populations, and almost everyone speaks Spanish. If you are in a large facility, ask for a medical interpreter to help you understand the forms and procedures.

**¿Qué tipo de análisis me van a hacer?**
keh TEE-po theh ah-NAH-lee-sees meh bahn ah-SEHR

What kind of test are you going to run?

**Mi tipo sanguíneo es...**
mee TEE-po sahng-GHEE-neh-o ehs

My blood type is . . .

**¿Qué me pasa?** *(keh meh PAH-sah):* What's wrong with me?

Certainly anyone who receives a diagnosis of something serious will get a second opinion, and you would want to do so even more if you aren't getting the diagnosis in English. For lesser, non–life threatening situations you may want to clearly understand what to do and not do in order to recover more quickly. Follow-up visits may be necessary if your stay is long enough. If you are really confused about any medical issue and need to get attention quickly, ask for a medical interpreter. Many of the doctors in large city hospitals received their education in the United States.

| | |
|---|---|
| **¿Cuándo debo volver a verle?** | When should I come back to see you? |
| KWAHN-do THEH-bo bol-BEH rah BEHR-leh | |
| **¿Debo ver a un especialista?** | Should I see a specialist? |
| DEH-bo beh rah oo nehs-peh-see-ah-LEES-tah | |

## Chapter 13

# Emergencies

**¡Socorro!** *(so-KO-rro):* Help!

This chapter begins at the beach because so many English-speaking tourists head there during the winter months. Students converge on beaches during Spring break and crowd into hotels, bars, restaurants, tents, and vans. Any and all of these environments present their own set of dangers and temptations, all of which are increased under the influence of alcohol.

Many of these U.S. and Canadian visitors come from inland areas, and frankly, many do not have much experience with the sea, so they have too little respect for it. People who live around the sea know its dangers. If you follow basic water safety rules you will probably have no need for some of the phrases in this chapter, but there are some dangers that have a mind of their own.

**Deme un chaleco salvavidas.**
DEH-meh oon chah-LEH-ko sahl-
    bah-VEE-dahs

Give me a life preserver.

**Tengo calambres en el pie.**
TEHNG-go kah-LAHM-breh seh nehl
    pee-eh

I have cramps in my foot.

**¡Incendio!** *(een-SEHN-dee-o)*: Fire!

Remember that there are different classes of fires, depending on their cause of ignition, such as a spark or flame or a short in an electrical circuit, and the materials that are being consumed, such as chemicals, grease, oil, and paper. Often, if you don't know the source of a fire or what is burning, you are wise to leave it to professionals and concentrate on saving human lives.

Hotel fires, of course, are the biggest fire danger a tourist is likely to face, followed by fires on boats, which in the worst case will end up exposing the passengers to dangers from the water. For safety instructions about what to do in case of fire, read the signs or, rather, look at the diagrams and pictures posted in hotels.

It isn't paranoid to examine the floor you are on to find the exits, particularly if you are above the third floor. In an emergency, you might be doubly handicapped by smoke and by an inability to speak or understand Spanish, so be proactive! Another word for fire extinguisher is *extintor* (ehs-teen-TOR).

| | |
|---|---|
| **¡Llame a los bomberos!** | Call the fire department! |
| YAH-meh ah los bom-BEH-ros | |
| **¿Hay un apagafuegos a mano?** | Is there an extinguisher handy? |
| ay yoo nah-pah-gah-FWEH-go sah MAH-no | |

**He tenido un choque de automóvil.** *(eh teh-NEE-tho oon CHO-keh theh ow-to-MO-beel)*: I've had a car accident.

On the road and you have a fender bender? The Green Angels, Mexico's roadside help, will show up—eventually. If you are traveling in the deserts or other rural areas, it is wise to have plenty of water, at least a gallon per passenger, flares, blankets, first aid kits, and some dried foods. Once the authorities arrive and injuries are addressed, be circumspect about how much information you give beyond your name and other such vital information.

Whatever you do, try to be cooperative without admitting guilt or placing blame until you know exactly what is at stake. It is difficult to anticipate what you may need to say or not say. If things look serious, insist on calling your consulate. Mexico does not operate on the premise that you are innocent until proven guilty—quite the opposite. Her legal system is founded on the Napoleonic Code: you are guilty until you prove you are not. Even a fender bender can become an expensive affair, so you may need help from U.S. or Canadian authorities who know how to help you navigate these waters.

It is wise to get cell phone service in Mexico if you are going to be spending much time on the road. Read up on the weather conditions and the type of environment you are in. Think like a Boy Scout, or should we say, like a member of *Los Caballeros Aztecas*, "the Aztec Gentlemen" as they are known in Mexico. It sounds a bit quaint, but Mexicans are proud of their indigenous roots, and as this name shows, they often invoke nativism to instill positive values in their youth.

| | |
|---|---|
| **Se me pinchó la llanta.** | I have a flat tire. |
| seh meh peen-CHO lah YAHN-tah | |
| **Necesito la grúa remolque.** | I need a tow truck. |
| neh-seh-SEE-to lah GROO-ah | |
| rreh-MOL-keh | |

**Mi esposo ha sufrido un ataque al corazón.** *(mee ehs-PO-so ah soo-FREE-tho oo nah-TAH-keh ahl ko-rah-SON):* My husband has had a heart attack.

Some emergency phrases are sobering even to write. If you are traveling with someone who is in a high-risk group, discreetly bookmark this page and then move on.

Being able to state a problem quickly and clearly can save time, and that saves lives in all emergencies. Know the Spanish names of any medical conditions you or a member of your party might have, as well as the type of insurance coverage they have. Check with your provider before you travel so you don't have to learn anything under stress.

| | |
|---|---|
| **Llame a un médico en seguida.** | Call a doctor right away. |
| YAH-meh ah oo MEH-thee-ko ehn seh-GHEE-thah | |
| **No sé qué le pasa.** | I don't know what is wrong with |
| no SEH KEH leh PAH-sah | him/her. |

 **¿Hay un médico/una partera aquí?** *(ay yoo MEH-thee-ko/OO-nah pahr-TEH-rah ah-KEE):* Is there a doctor/midwife here?

Having a baby in Mexico? He or she will be a Mexican citizen, just as any baby born in the United States has U.S. citizenship. Contact your consulate if you have a baby so the right paperwork can be provided for returning with your bundle to the United States or Canada.

If you have your baby in a hospital, have the hospital provide help with filling out forms about your baby and you. Get an interpreter to assist you. If you are a hardy traveler and for some reason have your baby in a rural area, then be sure to get to civilization.

It might feel like the Old West—it might even *be* the Old West while you are there. I lived without electricity for a while. I sometimes return to that quaint but quiet way of life as a means of unplugging from modern bustle. Eventually, though, you will have to reenter the modern world, and it is unforgiving about paperwork and proper identification.

**Se le ha roto la bolsa de aguas.**    Her water has broken.
seh leh ah RRO-to lah BOL-sah
   theh AH-gwahs

**Está a punto de dar a luz.**    She is about to give birth.
ehs-TAH POON-to theh DAH rah loos

**Mi hijo/hija se cayó.** *(mee EE-ho/EE-ha seh kah-YO):* My son/daughter fell down.

Nothing hurts quite the same as seeing your kid take a spill. Usually it's nothing. Sometimes it turns out to be nothing—after a few stitches. The biggest risks kids face are accidents and the biggest cause of accidents is lack of supervision. Remember, when you go to Mexico, they are in a place that is unfamiliar to them as well.

Mexico's infrastructure is uneven, so you cannot assume, for instance, that manhole covers are on everyplace they should be or that guardrails are always secure and on all balconies and stairwells, or even that all water coming from a spout is drinkable. Kids, being curious as cats, like to explore, so either explore with them or keep them on a short tether.

**Tiene una lesión grave.**
Tee-EH-neh OO-nah leh-see-ON
   GRAH-beh

He/She has a bad gash.

**Dele algo para el dolor.**
DEH-leh AHL-go PAH-rah ehl do-LOR

Give him/her something for the pain.

**Mi padre/madre no puede respirar.** *(mee PAH-dreh/MAH-dreh no PWEH-theh rrehs-pee-RAHR):* My father/mother can't breathe.

Animated conversations can result in choking on food that has "gone down the wrong way" and unexpected allergic reactions can result in swollen breathing passages. Both situations are frightening for the person experiencing them, and both are usually treatable if someone responds quickly. The Heimlich maneuver is a good thing to know. Be sure you have the presence of mind to actually do it and do it right. If someone is prone to allergic reactions, take whatever medication you know has worked to relieve them.

If you have peanut allergies, be aware that peanuts are plentiful in Mexico. On the positive side, they are not used in as many sauces in Mexico as they are in Malaysia, so you probably don't need to worry about ingesting them accidentally. However, people who are very sensitive to peanuts should be aware that they are such a popular and inexpensive snack that in some places the scent of peanuts is inescapable. Of course, this is delightful if you aren't allergic and like them!

**Tiene algo en la garganta.**
tee-EH-neh AHL-go ehn lah
   gahr-GAHN-tah

He/She has something in his/her throat.

| | |
|---|---|
| **Es alérgico a los cacahuates/los camarones.** | He/She is allergic to peanuts/shrimp. |
| eh sah-LEHR-hee-ko ah los kah-kah-WHAH-tehs/los kah-mah-RO-nehs | |

 **Me han robado el coche/el pasaporte/la billetera.** *(meh ahn rro-BAH-tho ehl KO-cheh/ehl pah-sah-POR-teh/lah bee-yeh-TEH-rah):* My car/passport/wallet has been stolen.

Being careful, being aware of where you are and who is around you, and being just a little bit paranoid can help prevent thefts, pickpocketing, and muggings. Make it harder to steal your things and a thief will usually go on to easier prey. Still, if expensive items are conspicuously displayed, the temptation can become too great. In all the years I lived or traveled in Mexico, I was never the victim of a holdup or any other form of thievery. One reason, besides good luck, is because I never dressed or acted like an easy mark. How do you act like someone who is not an easy mark? By looking like you know where you are when you are lost, like you are expecting someone. In a pinch, even waving as if you see a friend will make a would-be pickpocket or mugger decide to go elsewhere.

| | |
|---|---|
| **Vi/No vi al delincuente.** | I saw/did not see the perpetrator. |
| BEE/no bee ahl deh-leeng-KWEHN-teh | |
| **Había uno/más de uno.** | There was one./There were more than one. |
| ah-BEE-ah OO-no/MAHS theh OO-no | |

**¿Alguien sabe los primeros auxilios?** *(ahl-GHEE-ehn SAH-beh los pree-MEH-ro sah-ook-SEE-lee-os):* Does anyone know first aid?

If you don't know basic first aid, you should. Take a class at the Red Cross, the YMCA, or a local hospital or clinic. Even if you do know first aid, accidents will happen when you don't have your first aid kit with you and you'll need to ask for equipment or some form of assistance.

My first experience with Mexican health care involved being kindly pressed into service by an ambulance driver, who inexplicably had come alone to the home of an elderly man with a sprained ankle. He needed to take him to the hospital and, with the help of the old man's elderly wife, was able to put him on a stretcher. It looked like it had been at the Battle of Verdun: canvas with two poles, right on the ground. She couldn't pick up her end and so I was hailed to help pick him up and slide him into the ambulance onto a dusty cushion that looked like it used to be a mattress. He looked at me, told me what had happened, and instructed me to come back to the house later that evening. I did, wondering what was up.

I was handsomely paid for my services, but not by the health care system. The old couple rented me a room with a separate entrance, a shower (no hot water—what for?—it was always hot), a bed (with fresh sheets every day), a dresser, and a table and chair, for the hearty sum of $35 for the summer—provided I patch the wall so the iguanas would not come in. Oh, and I had to sit with them at breakfast and read the newspaper.

| | |
|---|---|
| **Necesitamos una ambulancia.** | We need an ambulance. |
| neh-seh-see-TAH-mo SOO-nahm boo-LAHN-see-ah | |
| **No puedo/puede caminar.** | I/He/She can't walk. |
| no PWEH-tho/PWEH-theh kah-mee-NAHR | |

# Chapter 14

# Making Plans

**¿A qué hora comienza?** *(ah keh O-rah ko-mee-EHN-sa):* What time does it start?

I'm sure everyone has heard of being on "island time" or "Latin time." There is some truth to the notion of Latin time, in the sense that people from Anglo or other northern European cultures will perceive Latins as being more laid-back and less precisely "on the dot" when it comes to appointments. Then there is the *siesta,* a very civilized custom that helps to break up an otherwise fast-paced life. Mexicans tend to eat their largest meal in the early afternoon and take it easy for a while afterwards; some even take a short nap and then return to work. In big cities, and for people in some professions, the *siesta* is just not feasible.

If you are on vacation, you will certainly discover that if you need to do certain types of errands, such as a shoe repair, you will not likely find the shop open from around one or two in the afternoon until around three or four. In other words, count on a two-hour slowdown in the pace of life in the early afternoon.

**El concierto comienza tarde.**    The concert begins late.
ehl kon-see-EHR-to ko-mee-EHN-sa
   TAHR-deh

**La exhibición se abre temprano.**    The exhibition opens early.
lah ehk-see-bee-see-ON seh
   AH-breh tehm-PRAH-no

 **¿Cómo se llega hasta allá?** *(KO-mo seh YEH-gahs tah YA):*
How can I get there?

Plan your trip to any time sensitive event with enough time to get lost and then find your way again. Using a map, asking for directions from hotel staff, or even making an appointment with a cabbie who has driven you somewhere before are good ways to lessen the anxiety of getting to an event with a scheduled beginning or a tour with a scheduled departure.

The first thing I do wherever I travel is get a local map and note the location of my hotel or other accommodations. Take your bearings; learn where the cabs and buses are. Get the lay of the land by doing some basic reconnoitering upon arrival and you won't need to ask for directions as often. By doing some quick homework, you also won't look quite as lost when you are lost. Besides, if you know a little about where you are, when you meet that friendly and hospitable Mexican who just does not want to admit that he really doesn't know where you are going, you'll be able to tell, thank him kindly, and then either figure it out yourself or get a second opinion.

**¿El hotel ofrece transporte gratis?**    Does the hotel offer free
ehl o-TEHL o-FREH-seh trahns-                transportation?
   POR-teh GRAH-tees

**Se puede ahorrar compartiendo**     We can save by sharing a cab.
   **un taxi.**

seh PWEH-theh ah-o-RRAHR
   kom-pahr-tee-EHN-do oon
   TAHK-see

**¿Todavía hay tiempo para llegar?** *(to-thah-BEE-yay tee-EHM-po PAH-rah yeh-GAHR):* Is there still time to get there?

If you are in a hurry, which you can usually avoid by planning well and building in extra time for the unexpected—and your own mis-judgments due to unfamiliar surroundings—you might need to tell people to step on it a bit. Remember that no one likes to be rushed, and Mexicans are no exception. In fact, it isn't an exaggeration to say that they probably take it less well than their northern neighbors. Mexicans go out of their way to avoid personal confrontations. When a Mexican is told to get a move on, particularly by a stranger, it could result in a passive-aggressive response. A cabbie, for instance, might just get lost or make a wrong turn.

So the lesson is, if you are in a rush, don't act like it. You can say you're in a hurry without sounding like you're in a hurry. And if you are not in a hurry, it is also good to let a Mexican know; Anglos too have a stereotype and part of it involves being always in a rush, being workaholics, and not knowing how to just relax. Mexicans don't gen-erally view the wild-and-crazy tourist as someone who is relaxing, but rather as someone on a binge of excess.

**Tengo prisa para salir/llegar.**　　I'm in a hurry to leave/get there.
TEHNG-go PREE-sah PAH-rah
　　sah-LEER/yeh-GAHR

**Tranquilo, hay mucho tiempo.**　　It's OK, there's plenty of time.
trang-KEE-lo ay MOO-cho
　　tee-EHM-po

**¿Podría recomendarme algo?** *(po-DREE-ah rreh-ko-mehn-DAHR-meh AHL-go):* Could you recommend something to me?

Sometimes it can feel good to relinquish the driver's seat when it comes to vacation plans. There is an interesting scene in the famous Spanish novel *Don Quixote*—not Mexican, I know—in which Don Quixote decides that the essence of seeking adventures is to let his horse decide which way to go.

Something can be learned from the adventure-seeking method of a literary knight-errant. If you are on your own, flipping a coin to decide might work—there is no one with you to tell you that you chose badly. Then again, the problem with a coin is that you have to decide to actually do what it says! If you're in a group, one way to have a laid-back trip is to let everyone have their day, or afternoon, to decide where you'll go and what you'll do. All you really need to do is have viable alternatives—a list of activities—and know their cost, in time and money.

If you don't have a focused idea of what you want to do in Mexico, this relaxed approach can actually let you open up to experience the place and the people. Even if you are focused on a goal, such as diving at a certain reef or seeing a specific museum or group of ruins, you can have vacations within the vacation, to keep receptive to new experiences. Following a whim that isn't truly dangerous can be enlightening. And isn't recharging your imaginative batteries one thing a vacation can do for you?

**¿Qué piensa usted de esto?**     What do you think of this?
keh pee-EHN-sah oos-TEHD theh
   EHS-to

 **¿Podría decir que me lo recomendó?** *(po-DREE-ah theh-SEER keh meh lo rreh-ko-mehn-DO)*: May I say you recommended it to me?

*Personalismo,* roughly but imperfectly translated as "a personal touch," is a characteristic of the Latin world in general. One does not do business with strangers. In the Anglo world, the prevailing attitude is that one ought not do business with friends, or mix business and pleasure. Anglos roll up their sleeves with total strangers as long as they agree that something is to their mutual benefit. They may or may not become friends, but that is irrelevant.

The prevailing attitude in the Latin world is that one does not do business with people one does not like, for personal, religious, cultural reasons, you name it. Becoming friends in the Latin world involves a sense of trust and that stems mostly from what two people have in common. That idea seems logical enough, but Anglo businesspeople often have a hard time being patient in a traditional Latin setting while a potential buyer or supplier in the Latin world wants to spend some time—days, perhaps longer—finding out just who the person is who has come with a business proposal.

If you are in Mexico on business, be ready to be asked personal questions of the sort that might even be illegal in a job interview in the United States or seem like an irrelevant waste of time. Questions

123

about family, educational background, religion, hobbies, you name it, are fair game. The social rituals are a bit like a courtship. Coming back without closing a deal is not the end of the world; it could mean that they are taking you very seriously and just need to sleep on it a bit: *consultar con la almohada* (kon-sool-TAHR kon lah ahl-mo-AH-thah). The bigger the deal, the closer the relationship, the longer and more involved the courtship.

**¿Conoce usted al dueño/a los**    Do you know the owner/employees?
**empleados?**
ko-NO-seh oos-TEHD ahl DWEHN-yo/
   ah lo sehm-pleh-AH-thos

**¿Les interesaría a los niños?** *(le seen-teh-reh-sah-REE-ah los NEEN-yos):* Would this be interesting to children?

Kids, teens included, are tough to entertain from time to time on most vacations. Every parent knows that even when a vacation is all about them, kids can get bored, over-stimulated, disappointed, you name it. I suspect that overstimulation is often at the root of most vacation blues, followed by disappointment: expectations were built too high and the reality didn't fit.

As with adults, finding or being shown the unexpected and experiencing variety will often cure the blues. Many adults go to Mexico with ideas in their heads about Old Mexico, formed from stereotypes in movies or dime-store novels. What they encounter is a complex civilization whose people live in many bands on a wide spectrum of assimilation, or lack thereof, into the industrialized world. This fact alone can often be a source of constant wonder and bewilderment. Observant and curious people really have no excuse for getting bored in Mexico. Over-stimulated and worn out, frustrated, yes, but never bored.

Mexicans love kids and they have large families, so if movies are your kids' thing, it is likely that there are many movies for them to pick from on a given night. On the other hand, the novelty of going to an open-air market is such that many kids are intrigued.

Depending on the length of your stay and type of accommodations, it is also possible that your child or children will begin to socialize with Mexicans their age. This can be the beginning of a serious interest in and respect for others and their cultures. Just remember that Mexicans take friendship, and visits to their home or to yours, very seriously. If, when you leave, you say you'll be in touch or that you'll write, follow through. Among Mexicans, people from the United States have a reputation for not keeping their word when they say such things. When you make contact again from up north, you'll be doing a lot to improve our neighborly relationship.

| | |
|---|---|
| **¿Es la película buena para los niños?** | Is the movie suitable for children? |
| ehs lah peh-LEE-koo-lah BWEH-nah PAH-rah los NEEN-yos | |
| **¿Se permite entrar a los niños?** | Are children allowed to enter? |
| seh pehr-MEE-teh en-TRAHR ah los NEEN-yos | |

**¿Hay que comprar los boletos de antemano?** *(ay keh kom-PRAHR los bo-LEH-tos theh ahn-teh-MAH-no):* Do you have to buy tickets in advance?

Mexicans just don't line up for things the way Anglos do. If you have to go to a window for service in many places, other than banks, airports, or other such establishments where there is traffic control with roped off areas for people to flow through, you may feel the crush of people all thinking they arrived first.

The lesson is, if you can buy tickets in advance of any event, and avoid having to figure out the logic of the pressing crowds around the ticket window, do. You'll then only have to deal with getting through the other pressing crowd of those who also have tickets.

Go to a bullfight, not for the spectacle of the tormented bovine, but to do people watching. You'll see the culture working by its own rules in crowds. What you see there among the people is more important than what you may learn about the bull or the prowess of the *torero*. What you learn you can apply to other places.

**¿Hay boletos todavía para el concierto?**
ay bo-LEH-tos to-thah-BEE-ah PAH-rah ehl kon-see-EHR-to

Are there still tickets for the concert?

**Queremos los mejores asientos.**
keh-REH-mos los meh-HO-reh sahs-see-EHN-tos

We want the best seats.

¿**Desea usted acompañarnos?** *(deh-SEH-ah oos-TEH dah-kom-pahn-YAHR-nos):* Do you want to go with us?

If you show some hospitality in Mexico as a guest, you'll be richly rewarded in friendship. Generally, Anglos have some trouble knowing how to receive and accept the warm hospitality offered to them there. However, if you have made a friend in Mexico, you have made a friend. Invite him or her to accompany you to something. It doesn't matter if it is big or small, so long as it corresponds in some measure to the level of the friendship or favor you may have been shown. In general, it is good to do as they do: start out small. Repaying favors is often how friendships start, there as anywhere. Genuineness is the key.

| | |
|---|---|
| **Usted ha sido tan amable, lo quiero invitar.** | You have been so nice, I'd like to invite you. |
| oos-TEHD ah SEE-tho tahn ah-MAH-bleh lo kee-EH-ro eem-bee-TAHR | |
| **Lo invito a cenar antes.** | Let me invite you to dinner before. |
| lo eem-VEE-to ah seh-NAHR AHN-tehs | |

¿**Es posible caminar hasta allá?** *(ehs po-SEE-bleh kah-mee-NAH rahstah-YAH):* Is it possible to walk there?

When you haven't planned in advance or discover a great opportunity to do something and need to make plans to get there in time, locals—for instance, your host or hotel information desk—are your lifeline.

Unlike people in the United States, most Mexicans still know the art of walking to places. Although diesel and cooking smells dominate the rush hour effluvia that dance on one's nostrils, and it is too true that cars are everywhere and pollution is often terrible even in coastal towns, if walking is a feasible option, Mexicans are less averse to walking than Anglos.

| | |
|---|---|
| **¿Cuál autobús debo tomar para llegar a tiempo?** | Which bus should I take to get there in time? |
| KWAH lah-o-to-BOOS theh-bo to-MAHR PAH-rah yeh-GAH rah tee-EHM-po | |

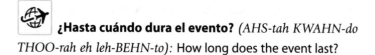

**¿Hasta cuándo dura el evento?** *(AHS-tah KWAHN-do THOO-rah eh leh-BEHN-to)*: How long does the event last?

Mexican cities have a lot of nightlife, and not just for young, single people. Professionals have had a siesta or a break in the middle of the day. They have gone home and had a bite. Even the middle class has servants, so the children are looked after and many couples go to their favorite places to eat, dance, chat, do business, or just relax.

It is difficult to get into the local scene without language skills or connections, but fortunately for the tourist with such interests, many Mexicans in tourist cities such as Mazatlán, Puerto Vallarta, Ixtapa, or Acapulco on the Pacific coast, or Cozumel on the Gulf, will also go to the clubs the tourists go to, in addition to the ones that only locals seem to know. Cost tends to keep out the working class, so the local clientele is mostly well-to-do by Mexican standards. As is true anywhere, the fast track to getting into locals-only establishments is membership in international societies, professional organizations, and fraternal organizations.

The Mexicans in Mazatlán go clubbing in the same places as the tourists, but they also have clubs and other restaurants that only locals seem to know about. They are not as rich looking, but they are the real item. When you meet locals in tourist spots, you can find out how to get into the local scene.

| | |
|---|---|
| **¿Hay restaurantes abiertos después?** | Are there any restaurants open afterward? |
| ay rrehs-tah-oo-RAHN-teh sah-bee-EHR-tos dehs-PWEHS | |
| **¿Adónde vamos después?** | Where shall we go afterward? |
| ah-THON-deh BAH-mos dehs-PWEHS | |

# Chapter 15

## Keeping in Touch

**Ha sido un placer conocerlo/la.** *(ah SEE-thoh oom plah-SEHR ko-no-SEHR-lo/lah):* It's been a pleasure to meet you.

Mexicans, and indeed most of the nations that are heirs to the Greco-Roman cultures, are very conscious of social graces. These formulae are what grease the wheels of society, and forgetting them can instantly oxidize what otherwise would have been a good relationship.

Even the relative relaxation of moving from the formal use of *usted* to the familiar *tú* does not obviate the need to continue observing social niceties. In fact, friendship brings with it certain assumptions.

If you become friends and truly intend to keep up the relationship, it will be important to know things like birthdays or saint's days (the day on the Roman Catholic calendar dedicated to the saint whose name the person bears), anniversaries, names of family members, and so on.

Since you are using a phrase book to make some social contacts, take heart in the fact that while Mexicans can be sticklers for etiquette, they are also quite forgiving of the foreigner who is trying and making obvious progress in his or her command of Spanish and social customs. They are genuinely pleased to hear any American really try to use Spanish.

| | |
|---|---|
| **Me gustaría seguir en contacto con usted.** | I would like to keep in touch with you. |
| meh goos-tah-REE-ah seh-GHEER ehn kon-TAHK-to ko noos-TEHD | |
| **Creo que es el comienzo de una relación duradera.** | I think this is the beginning of a lasting relationship. |
| KREH-o keh eh sehl ko-mee-EHN-so theh OO-nah rreh-lah-see-ON doo-rah-THEH-rah | |

**Que no perdamos el contacto, ¿eh?** *(keh no pehr-DAH-mo sehl kon-TAHK-to eh):* Let's not lose touch, OK?

Give an encouraging word to let the other person know that you have been glad to meet them and would like to keep up. Visitors from the United States are viewed as people who come to Mexico and seem to be striking up a friendship, but don't follow through.

One of my Mexican friends, a fellow professor, related an interesting anecdote about how he learned to not necessarily trust the veracity of what Americans say when it comes to what in his culture are friendship-making overtures. When he came to the United States, he could speak English reasonably well and he became friendly with an American guy at an on-campus job. This was in the early 80s and the young American said "let's do lunch sometime." My friend got out his daily planner and started flipping through it to see when he might be free. When he looked up, he saw an uncomfortable look on the guy's face that made it plain that he had only said it as casually as we say "How are you?" or "Good morning."

| | |
|---|---|
| **Al llegar a casa, le mandaré un mensaje.** | When I get home, I'll send you a message. |
| ahl yeh-GHA rah KAH-sah leh mahn-dah-REH oom mehn-SAH-heh | |
| **¿Tiene usted un teléfono celular?** | Do you have a cell phone? |
| tee-EH-neh oos-TEHD oon teh-LEH-fo-no seh-loo-LAHR | |

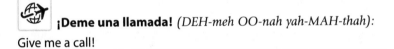

**¡Deme una llamada!** *(DEH-meh OO-nah yah-MAH-thah):* Give me a call!

This is what you should say if your Mexican friend or friends speak English well enough to leave a message or have another friend who can do so. Nowadays, with the potential for face-to-face conversations via Internet in real time, even when both people do not speak each other's languages very well, a lot can be negotiated. Speaking on the phone is tough. You cannot see gestures and expressions or figure out the timing and pauses.

If you know you're going to be on the phone for making plans, you should script yourself so you can provide information for the Spanish speaker. It is not a good idea for the Mexican to expect you to be able to understand his or her free-flowing prose about when and where to meet, so if you can, at least take charge by being the one saying when and where to meet or arrange pickups.

**Éste es el número de mi oficina/casa/celular.**

EHS-tehs ehl NOO-meh-ro theh mee o-fee-SEE-nah/KAH-sah/seh-loo-LAHR

This is my office/home/cell phone number.

**Le llamo para que pueda captar mi número.**

leh YAH-mo PAH-rah keh PWEH-thah kahp-TAHR mee NOO-meh-ro

I'll call you so you can capture my number.

**Déjeme un mensaje de voz.** *(DEH-heh-meh oom mehn-SAH-heh theh BOS):* Leave me a voice message.

If you get a voice message on, say, your hotel phone, you can almost certainly find someone on the hotel staff to interpret it for you. Otherwise, it is important to tell your friend before he or she plans to leave a message that it needs to deal with the bare bones of how you are going to hook up later.

If you are a business traveler, you can probably count on having a Spanish-speaking coworker with you (your company *did* think of the very real problem of the language barrier when it decided to send you to Mexico, didn't it?). If not, the Mexican businesspeople can send faxes, messages, and so forth to your home office, where surely your company will find professional translators and interpreters to deal with any official business, such as contracts, that needs to cross language barriers.

**Mi socio sabe español y podrá interpretarlo.**
My partner knows Spanish and can interpret it.

mee SO-see-o SAH-behs pan-YOL ee po-DRAH een-tehr-preh-TAHR-lo

**Yo le mandaré el contrato por fax.**
I'll fax you the contract.

ee-YO leh mahn-dah-REHL kon-TRAHK-to por fahks

**¿Me podría dar su número de teléfono/fax?** *(meh po-DREE-ah dahr soo NOO-meh-ro theh teh-LEH-fo-no/fahks)*: Would you give me your phone/fax number?

From a Mexican point of view, Anglos get down to business too quickly, but if you are at the stage where real business can at least be anticipated, it is appropriate to exchange business cards and contact information. There is sometimes a bit of flair to this process, and Mexicans often take great pride in their business cards, which can be humorous, witty, artistic . . . you name it. They tend to put a great deal of thought into how their card stands for what they do. So admire their card as you would their choice of car, suit, wine, or other fine consumer good.

Of course, it is important to let your Mexican host, acquaintance, or business counterpart, your *homólogo* (o-MO-lo-go), know how to get in touch with you while you are in Mexico, when you'll be returning home, and other details that could impact deadlines and meeting times.

**Aquí tiene usted mi tarjeta.**
Here is my card.

ah-KEE tee-EH-neh oos-TEHD mee tahr-HEH-tah

135

**Puede llamarme al hotel.**
PWEH-theh yah-MAHR-meh ah
  lo-TEHL

You can call me at the hotel.

**¿Tiene usted acceso al Internet?** *(tee-EH-neh oos-TEH ahk-SEH-so ah leen-tehr-NEH):* Do you have Internet access?

Most hotels with a few stars have Internet access, so if you take your laptop you'll be in touch with everyone you ever would be. If you are trying to get in touch with people back home, be aware of time zone differences. Sometimes these are not as logical as they should be. For instance, Ciudad Juárez and El Paso are an hour apart when Texas goes on daylight saving time.

When you check into a hotel planning to use your laptop, be sure to also ask if the Internet connection is included, or you may have a surprise on your bill. Just as in the United States, if you connect to the Internet via the hotel's television, you will almost certainly incur some sort of charge.

**¿La tarifa incluye la conexión al Internet?**
lah tah-REE-fah eeng-KLOO-yeh lah
  ko-nek-see-ON ahl een-tehr-NEH

Does the bill include the Internet connection?

**Tengo acceso a mi cuenta desde el hotel.**
TEHNG-go ahk-SEH-so ah mee
  KWEHN-tah dehs-thehl o-TEHL

I have access to my account from the hotel.

**¿Hay un café con Internet cerca de aquí?** *(ah-yoong kah-FEH ko neen-tehr-NEH SEHR-kah theh ah-KEE):* Is there an Internet café around here?

Most major hotels have some sort of complimentary business facilities or are Internet ready in the room, either via wireless or through the TV (which will almost always involve an extra charge, just as in the United States or Canada). You might prefer the ambience of an Internet café away from your hotel room where, for a cup of coffee or perhaps an additional nominal fee, you can hook up your own PC or use any they might provide.

 **¿Cuándo está disponible para hablar en una sala de charla?** *(KWAHN-do ehs-TAH dees-po-NEE-bleh PAH-rah ah-BLAH-reh NOO-nah SAH-lah theh CHAHR-lah):* When are you available to talk in a chat room?

Even if your conversational skills are limited, you can learn a lot by participating in a chat room or in more controlled settings, provided you are in one with someone you already know. Spanish-language chat rooms are inhabited by the same sorts of lounge lizards that infest the English-speaking world. There is almost nothing in them of linguistic value unless you are a linguistic anthropologist studying the demise of civilization.

All these negatives become positives, however, if you are in a chat with someone who genuinely wants to communicate in written Spanish and you, too, genuinely want to learn. In e-mail or chat, you have the luxury of time to answer and the time can be used to look things up.

**Mi identidad en la sala es...**     My chatroom ID is . . .
mee thehn-tee-THAH thehn lah
   SAH-lah ehs

**¿Es usted miembro de alguna red social?** *(eh-soos-TEHD mee-EHM-bro theh ahl-GOO-nah RREHD so-see-AHL):* Are you a member of any social network?

Light years from the typical chat room environment are social networks. These environments are where professionals link up and people find jobs. They find future love interests and old friends—and make new ones. If you indicate an interest, some networks will find or suggest people to link with. This feature can lead you to other English speakers who are interested in Mexico, whether for business or for pleasure, as well as Spanish speakers who are interested in helping with Spanish in exchange for help with English. It is better than any pen-pal relationship you may have had once upon a time.

It takes a little creativity to craft a profile and indicate interests that will attract just what you are looking for when it comes to Spanish language or Mexico. The general rule is to be as specific as you can so that the people who seek to link with you are more likely to be a good match. While in Mexico you have a potential audience of people with whom to link, particularly if you are there on business.

**Yo le mandaré una invitación/**     I'll send you an invitation/link to
   **el enlace al sitio.**            the site.
ee-YO leh mahn-dah-REH OO-nah
   eem-bee-tah-see-ON/
   ehn-LAH-seh ahl SEE-tee-o

**¿Cómo prefiere que me comunique con usted?** *(KO-mo preh-fee-EH-reh keh meh ko-moo-NEE-keh ko noos-TEHD):* How do you prefer I contact you?

Finally, let's not forget that there is such a thing as snail mail, called *correo de caracol* in Spanish, or sometimes *correo de burro*—mule mail! I have sometimes had difficulty doing business with folks in Mexico when I needed to send a physical document or object that couldn't be faxed. Some locations (or specific businesses) are served better, or even exclusively, by one type of overnight carrier.

If you are truly on vacation and plan to be totally disconnected from the Internet (good for you!), but find you simply have to use it, there are Internet cafés and, of course, some hotels will have a courtesy room or a business facility where you may find a connection, perhaps included in your room charge, perhaps not.

**¿Cuál es su dirección de correo electrónico/de caracol?**
KWAH-leh soo thee-rehk-see-ON deh ko-RREH-o eh-lehk-TRO-nee-ko/theh kah-rah-KOL

What is your e-mail/snail-mail address?

# Chapter 16

# Weather

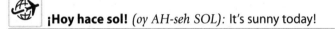 **¡Hoy hace sol!** *(oy AH-seh SOL):* It's sunny today!

The Aztecs worshiped *Queztalcoatl,* their creator god, whose visible manifestation was the sun. In that sunny place another god occasionally makes his presence known, and with devastating results: *Huracán.*

In contrast with the extremes of drought, intense heat, and occasional dust storms of the northern deserts and the muggy, often breezeless heat of the south and ocean coasts, Mexico's mountainous regions and central valley are more temperate. In some upper elevations the temperatures are even good for grape cultivation. These elevations are subject to hard frost and even snow, mostly above the populated areas.

Mexicali, a small city next to the California border near Arizona, is so hot in the summers that the Mexicans have a little joke about it. When a person from Mexicali goes to hell, he takes a blanket!

**¡Qué buen/mal tiempo hace!**     What great/rotten weather!

keh BWEHN/MAHL tee-EHM-po

   AH-seh

**Está lloviendo muy fuerte.** *(ehs-TAH yo-bee-EHN-do MOO-ee FWEHR-teh):* It's raining very hard.

In desert regions, a sudden downpour can be deadly, since they can fill the upper elevations of many dry river beds, known also in the American Southwest as *arroyos* (ah-RRO-yos) and cause flash flooding that can turn trucks on their sides.

People can be quickly swept away in the fast-moving shallow water and, unable to stand, often drown in ridiculously shallow torrents. The moral of the story is don't camp in an *arroyo;* don't park your vehicle in one, and don't count on sunny skies to stay sunny, even in the desert. The moist winds from the Pacific and the Gulf can bring a lot of moisture, which cools and condenses as it rises into the hills and then can fall faster than the ground can absorb it.

Those warnings aside, the deserts, both low-lying and high elevation, are beautiful places. I remember driving once through driving snow in April in Chihuahua through terrain identical to that surrounding El Paso, Texas, and Carlsbad, New Mexico. It didn't stick for long, but it was at once breathtaking and dangerous to drive in due to poor visibility and the ice on the blacktop. It ended as unexpectedly as it had begun. Be ready for a few surprises in the weather. The central region of Mexico is a bit like a warmer version of the U.S. Midwest. As Mark Twain said, if you don't like the weather, wait ten minutes.

**Estará cerrado el aeropuerto, ¿no?**   The airport is probably closed, isn't it?
ehs-tah-RAH seh-RRAH-tho eh
　　lah-eh-ro-PWEHR-to no

**Con esta tormenta, no podemos**   With this storm, we can't sail.
**navegar.**
ko NEHS-tah tor-MEHN-tah no
　　po-THEH-mos nah-beh-GAHR

**¿Qué tiempo va a hacer mañana?** *(keh tee-EHM-po bah*
*SEHR mahn-YAH-nah):* What's tomorrow's weather look like?

While local anomalies can be surprising and cannot always be predicted by the big picture given by satellite images, weather forecasts
are very useful for making plans in general. Odd moments at the local
level are mostly rare events of short duration, even if they are a bit
unnerving or dangerous.

If you are an experienced sailor, camper, or hiker in the United
States, much of what you know will still apply, obviously, but some
fine-tuning will still be in order. Yachtsmen will need to know about
local conditions, currents, and other phenomena caused by weather
around the Tropic of Cancer. Hikers and campers need to learn about
flora and fauna that can help them in times of emergency or kill them
if they are careless, unprepared, or just plain unlucky. If you have not
hiked in desert conditions, you have much to learn before you venture into an environment so hot, harsh, and dry that it mummifies the
ones who don't come home.

I used to live and work in the desert. I would walk a mile from
my home to an office and drink a liter of water both ways and still
be thirsty when I got there. Sweat often evaporates before it can
dampen your clothes. In other words, the water hardly has a chance

to go "through you" as it does in other places, so you need a lot of it. And without replenishing salts, you can be in just as bad a shape as if you had no water.

**Si hace buen tiempo, vamos a tomar el sol.**
see AH-seh BWEHN tee-EHM-po BAH-mo sah to-MAH rehl SOL

If the weather is nice, we're going to sunbathe.

**Si no hace buen tiempo, ¿qué podremos hacer?**
see no AH-seh BWEHN tee-EHM-po keh po-DREH-mo sah-SEHR

If it's not nice out, what can we do?

 **Va a llover pronto.** *(bah yo-BEHR PRON-to):* It's going to rain soon.

If you're out on the water or on a trail you may see a dark, angry cloud on the horizon and will then need to look for a protected cove, anchor, or find shelter. Mexico has some tremendously powerful thunderstorms, like many places of similar terrain in the U.S. Southwest or the Great Plains.

Lightning strikes are a very real possibility if you are in open country or on the water, so pay attention not just to forecasts, but keep your eyes open as well. If you are in a city, such storms will often mean a black- or brownout and other disruptions of basic services. Unlike in the United States or Canada, sometimes those disruptions become a part of daily routine for far longer than you would wish.

**¿Estamos en la temporada**
   **de lluvias?**

Are we in the rainy season?

ehs-TAH-mo sehn lah tehm-po-
   RAH-thah theh YOO-bee-ahs

**¿Será seguro navegar en barco de vela?** *(seh-RAH seh-GOO-ro nah-beh-GAH rehm BAHR-ko theh BEH-lah):* Is it safe to go sailing?

If you are an experienced boatman or boatwoman, you don't need any advice about what to do when you are out on the water, but you might need a little help talking to people about conditions before you set sail. One thing I noticed about Mexican fishermen and operators of pleasure craft is that they often underestimate the dangers because they need to make a living. If the weather looks threatening, use your better judgment and wait for ideal conditions.

**El tiempo está feo; regresemos**
   **a puerto.**

The weather is nasty; let's put back
   to port.

ehl tee-EHM-po ehs-TAH FEH-o
   rreh-greh-SEH-mo sah PWEHR-to

**¿Podemos anclar hasta que pase**
   **la tormenta?**

Can we anchor until the storm
   passes?

po-THEH-mo sahng-KLAH RAHS-tah
   keh PAH-seh lah tor-MEHN-tah

**¿Cuándo va a escampar?** *(KWAHN-do bahs-kahm-PAHR):* When is this rain going to let up?

Let's say you're temporarily huddled with a lot of other folks waiting for a storm to pass or feel stuck in your hotel because of a rainstorm that seemed like it would pass. How soon will it be over? Most likely, the locals will be familiar enough with their weather that they will be able to say what is likely, in the absence of a bona-fide weather report.

If your Internet is working, you probably won't need to ask anyone about the weather because you'll be able to surf over to satellite images to get a big picture of what is happening. If not, a recent newspaper will carry the weather and, fortunately, the weather page is loaded with intuitive, mostly universal symbols and so forth to help you get a handle on where the current situation fits into the scheme of things.

While you are waiting in your room for a storm to pass, use the time to plan your next outing, or alter the plans you had made for the day if the weather looks like it is going to cancel them.

Mexicans, particularly the young people, love a sudden cloudburst in the middle of the hot summer. I remember one June night in Mazatlán when the clubs emptied out into the street as soon as word of the downpour made it into the discos. The partygoers came running out in their finest clothes to get soaked and enjoy the drop in temperature. The cloudburst was accompanied by a blackout that lasted an hour or so. Several smaller merchants, particularly the ones with grilling operations, had generators up and running in no time and made a handsome bit of change while people were waiting for the lights to return to the dance floors.

**La tormenta será intensa pero breve.**

lah tor-MEHN-tah seh-RAH
een-TEHN-sah PEH-ro BREH-beh

The storm will be intense but brief.

**¡Está granizando!**

Ehs-TAH grah-nee-SAHN-do

It's hailing!

**¿Qué dice el barómetro?** *(keh THEE-sehl bah-RO-meh-tro):*
What is the barometer reading?

In some cases, pilots and fishermen may need real readings of weather phenomena even more than yachtsmen and other pleasure boaters. Fish bite when there is a low-pressure system—at least freshwater fish. Sportsmen of other types may want to know just how *hot* is hot or how cold it might get out on the desert at night.

If you are a sportsman or sportswoman, a spelunker, a rock climber, or a pilot, knowing more exact details about weather and other conditions is often vital. If you anticipate needing more in-depth information of this sort, be sure to look up the names of the instruments so you can at least ask a tour guide or expedition team leader to take a look at the proper instrumentation.

**¿Cuánto calor hace?**

KWAHN-to kah-LO RAH-seh

How hot is it?

**¿De noche, no baja la temperatura mucho?**

deh NO-cheh no BAH-hah lah
tehm-peh-rah-TOO-rah MOO-cho

Doesn't the temperature drop a lot at night?

147

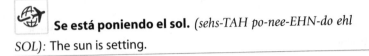 **Se está poniendo el sol.** *(sehs-TAH po-nee-EHN-do ehl SOL):* The sun is setting.

Maybe it's time for a sunset. If you are alone, you might look up how to invite someone to have a drink and share the sunset with them while sipping something with an umbrella in it.

If you are from a coastal area yourself, you know that some beaches smell great and others, especially at low tide, smell awful. It depends on the time of year. So if sunsets, especially romantic ones, are important to you, inquire about the best beaches or other vantage points for watching the sun set.

Naturally, if you are on the Gulf coast, you'll be watching sunrises. At that hour, it is unlikely that you'll be able to find one of those drinks with an umbrella in it. One popular place for locals in seaside towns and cities to stroll is called the *malecón* (mah-leh-KON), the name for the seawall, usually with a broad avenue that hugs the beach. It is usually elevated several feet as a breakwater, hence its name.

**Hace fresco ahora.**                It's chilly now.
AH-seh FREHS-ko ah-O-rah

 **No hay mucha visibilidad.** *(no ay MOO-chah bee-see-bee-lee-THAD):* There is not much visibility.

Pilots, mountain climbers, and hikers all know that visibility is even more important than temperature for safety reasons. Of course, if you're flying a major airline, you don't need to make decisions about flying, but many private pilots from the United States fly into smaller regional airports in Mexico and so it might be helpful to know how to make basic inquiries about conditions.

**No es seguro volar bajo estas condiciones.**

It's not safe to fly in these conditions.

no eh seh-GOO-ro bo-LAHR BAH-ho
    EHS-tahs kon-dee-see-O-nehs

**Esperemos hasta que escampe.**

Let's wait until the rain has stopped.

Ehs-peh-REH-mo SAHS-tah
    kehs-KAHM-peh

**¿Esta tormenta va a ser huracán?** *(EHS-tah tor-MEHN-tah bah seh roo-rah-KAHN):* Will this storm turn into a hurricane?

If you have ever been in a serious tropical storm, you know that there is a moment when it occurs to you to wonder if the storm they predicted yesterday and has now hit, knocking out electricity and cutting you off from the world, has been upgraded to hurricane status.

Many powerful storms have hit Mexican resort areas over the years, stranding tourists for a few days and causing the usual devastation and loss of life. As our own experience with hurricanes has shown, almost all loss of life is avoidable if people simply evacuate when they are told to do so.

Professionals in health care fields might consider volunteering for relief efforts if they find themselves in Mexico in the thick of a serious storm. Their work will always be appreciated and remembered.

**¿Nos van a evacuar?**

Are they going to evacuate us?

nos bah nah eh-bah-koo-AHR

**¿Cuál es el lugar más seguro durante un huracán?**

Where is the safest place during a hurricane?

KWAH leh sehl loo-GAHR mah
    seh-GOO-ro doo-RAHN-teh oo
    noo-rah-KAHN

# Chapter 17

# Sports and Gambling

¿**Qué actividades deportivas hay aquí?** *(KEH ak-tee-bee-THAH-thehs deh-por-TEE-ba sah-ee yah-KEE):* What sort of sports can I do here?

In search of sports? Mexico abounds in opportunities to explore hiking trails and ruins and to go reef diving, parasailing, deep-sea fishing, hunting, and fresh-water fishing. In addition, you can find the usual "organized" or indoor sports in many resorts, and most large towns now have a sports or fitness club.

Traditionally, exercise for its own sake, or even for fitness, is not something that has been practiced in the Latin world. Until recently, breaking a sweat has been regarded among the more affluent and educated youth as something that is done by people who have to work with their hands. Smoking is more common in the Latin world than in most parts of the United States (except for parts of the South).

Even today, the idea of putting on one's running outfit and going for a jog in an urban park is viewed as odd. There are places for exercise and these are not usually the places where people congregate socially. The beaches can be an exception, if for no other reason than the preponderance of U.S. and Canadian tourists who simply do things their own way.

**¿Hay un gimnasio en el hotel?**          Is there a gym in the hotel?
AH-yoon heem-NAH-see-o eh
 nehl o-TEHL

 **¡Gol!** *(GOL):* Goal!

Due to the rising popularity of soccer in the United States, by now everyone has heard the announcers at the World Cup yell *¡gol!*— often for so long one marvels at their lung capacity. *Fútbol,* not football, is the rage outside the United States. In fact, American football, while often admired by Latin Americans, is also viewed by many as a symbol of American excess and cultural isolationism. Never mind that the *fútbol* fans are just as nuts and often as unruly as any other sports crowd, including our British and Australian cousins, who can get pretty rowdy over rugby.

 In 1978 I spent an interesting month in Mazatlán, during which time I watched the World Cup in a bar. Argentina beat the Netherlands 3–1. I didn't learn much about soccer, but I did learn that the rest of the world does not play football. And that, for me, was the beginning of an education in cross-cultural communication. In fact, for most of that month I sat with another young guy from Japan who spoke no English, but whose Spanish was quite good. This amounted to another lesson about how English isn't always the language of command, to use the maritime term.

**¡Qué chévere/gacho!**          How great/lousy!
KEH CHEH-beh-reh/GAH-cho

**Me encanta el fútbol.** *(mehng KAHN-tah ehl FOOT-bol):* I love soccer.

Most Latin Americans seem to be more familiar with their national literati than people in the United States are with theirs. Likewise, over the past three decades I have noticed, albeit unscientifically, that Latin Americans whom one would never think follow sports will know a lot about their country's record in the World Cup. The Mexicans are most patriotic about *fútbol.* As is true with most team loyalties, they tend to be loyal to a team based on the place they themselves are from or identify with. It is highly regional. Sports at the national level constitute a sort of contained and controlled civil war.

Will the Cubs ever win the World Series? Cubs fans don't seem to let that stop them. The same is true in Mexico. One's team is one's team. As guest it is better to ask questions than to try to impress with knowledge of a sport your country isn't known for—unless, of course, you play soccer well. Then you're on your own because, like all sports, soccer has a culture among players and fans. If you don't know much, showing interest in *fútbol* or a local team can open doors to other social circles, and if not, at least earn you some respect for your openness.

**¿Adónde podemos ir para ver el partido?**
ah-THON-deh po-THEH-mo SEER
   PAH-rah BEH rehl pahr-TEE-tho

Where can we go to watch the game?

**¿Cuál cree usted que va a ganar?** *(KWAHL kreh oos-TEHD keh BAH ah gah-NAHR):* Which team do you think will win?

Whether you're in a bar or in a stadium watching a game of *fútbol,* you will be noticed and an object of some curiosity. It is your chance to be an ambassador of goodwill for your country. At any rate, your level of interest and enthusiasm will be noticed.

Just as at home, you might notice which side the spectators around you are cheering for. Sad but true, there can be belligerent fans in any culture. Since you're there to have a good time—and incidentally exemplify the best of your country—it is wise to be more Mexican than Mexicans when it comes to avoiding confrontation. A good way is to ask a genuine question or two now and then.

If you go to a game, it is likely that a day or two will go by between the time you buy the tickets and the game, or that you went to Mexico knowing you would possibly take in a game. Use that interim time to look up a few statistics and learn about the team if you're not already familiar with it. Not everyone around you will be totally incapable of speaking English. There are more Mexicans who know English than Americans who know Spanish. You might be able to converse in some depth with other fans. They'll be proud to show off their English, and you'll make a good impression if you know more than they expect.

| | |
|---|---|
| **Soy aficionado del equipo...** | I'm a . . . fan. |
| soy ah-fee-see-o-NAH-tho theh | |
|    leh-KEE-po | |
| **No sé mucho sobre el fútbol, pero** | I don't know a lot about soccer, but I |
|    **me encanta.** | really like it. |
| no SEH MOO-cho SO-breh ehl | |
|    FOOT-bol PEH-ro mehng KAHN-tah | |

✈ **¡Hay una pelea en la cancha!** *(ay yoo-nah peh-LEH-ah ehn lah CAHN-chah):* There's a fight on the field!

As you follow a game and events unfold, it is only natural to be engaged and curious—or why show up? At any rate, not all of what you see is going to be self-explanatory. Naturally, people around you occasionally are going to be puzzled and you just might be able to let them know what they missed when they blinked or were tuned out.

*Fútbol* is a fast paced game, like hockey or basketball, and is played on a large field. The prowess and agility of Pelé, the Brazilian player of a generation ago, triggered an upsurge in interest in soccer in this country. It's fair to say that without Pelé, soccer moms might be unknown. His work showed the world, particularly people in the United States, that soccer was a sport that required the fine-tuned skills of gymnastics, the strength and speed of football or hockey, and the precision of basketball. It can be electrifying to watch!

**¿Por qué dejaron de jugar?**      Why did they stop playing?
por KEH deh-HAH-ron deh hoo-GAHR

✈ **¡Vamos a jugar al billar!** *(BAH-mo sah hoo-GAH rahl bee-YAHR):* Let's play pool!

Pool is a game many people enjoy playing—one eye, mind, and hand—often while watching a physically demanding team sport on a large screen. Sports bars do exist in Mexico, too. I've played pool with guys from Mexico who seem almost never to miss, and yet the game remains for most of them a game. It's a quiet sort of honor for most Mexican guys who play pool simply to be known and respected among their *cuates* (koo-AH-tehs), or buddies, as a great pool player, not as a pool shark.

Not that those don't exist as well. Go to any bar in Mexico and you're just as likely to meet a guy who'll be glad to take your money after throwing a few games to make you think he's just desperate when he offers you great odds. Just remember that we call the high numbers *stripes,* whereas Mexicans call them the *grandes* (GRAHN-dehs), or *big ones* (i.e., big numbers), and what we call *solids* are the *chicas* (CHEE-kahs), or *little ones.* Just knowing that might earn you respect and make them think you know what you're doing.

| | |
|---|---|
| **¿Jugamos en parejas?** | Shall we play doubles? |
| hoo-GAH-mo sehn pah-REH-hahs | |
| **¿A quién le toca?** | Whose turn is it? |
| ah kee-EHN leh TO-kah | |

**¡Chelas, chavas y Chivas!** *(CHEH-lahs CHAH-bahs ee CHEE-bahs):* Beer, chicks, and the Chivas!

Now it's time to learn about enthusiasm, Mexican style. First off, *chelas* is the slang term for beer in Mexico. It's like saying *suds* or *brewskies* in English. *Chavas* means *chicks* (as in women)—no need to elaborate on that one. *Chivas,* literally *goats,* is the name of Guadalajara's soccer team. But that is just to whet your appetite. Are you ready to learn to do the universal Mexican cheer, one that works for local teams as well as national teams when competing internationally? Here you go:

| | |
|---|---|
| **Chiquitibum a la bim bom ba** | chee-kee-tee-boo mah lah beem boom BAH |
| **Chiquitibum a la bim bom ba** | chee-kee-tee-boo mah lah beem boom BAH |

| | |
|---|---|
| **A la bio; a la bao; a la bim bom ba** | ah lah BEE-o; ah lah BA-o; ah la beem bom BAH |
| **México, México, ¡ra, ra, ra!** | MEH-hee-ko, MEH-hee-ko, rah, rah, RAH |

If you know this cheer and can say it right, you'll be a hit in any sports crowd, but listen for it so you can be sure to get its rhythm down right. It doesn't really *mean* anything, as I think is obvious. It's just a cheer, a shout of rhythmic and rhyming enthusiasm.

I actually knew a guy who got a contract for a job because, after all else was said and done, he knew a famous poem by the national poet of another Latin American country. Little things, or maybe they aren't so little after all, can give you an edge.

| | |
|---|---|
| **¿Dónde puedo comprar esa camisa?** | Where can I buy that shirt? |
| DON-deh PWEW-tho kom-PRAHR EH-sah kah-MEE-sah | |
| **¿Podría hacer el favor de sacarnos la foto?** | Would you kindly take our picture? |
| po-DREE-ah SEH rehl fah-BOR deh sah-KAHR-nos lah FO-to | |

**¿Quién gana?** *(kee-EHN GAH-nah):* Who's winning?

You might want to know the score at a game in a stadium, but chances are you're just as aware of a scoreboard when you're in Mexico as when you are in the United States. You're more likely to need to ask this question if you're playing a game—unless the game is clearly for gambling purposes. Most Mexicans play games like we

157

do, for social or family reasons. Although some families can play some really cutthroat board games in the United States, and the same is true anywhere, you are probably not going to be an intimate part of a family in Mexico unless you already know them from a previous visit or unless you've met them in your country.

Playing a game with a guest is generally a gentle affair, an excuse to do something that truly is secondary to conversation and getting to know you. However, those who play the ancient and honorable game of *ajedrez* (ah-heh-DRES), or chess, might be an exception. If you like *dominó* (note the stress on the last syllable of the name of this game which, other than being singular in form, is the same as in English), you'll be in good company. While it seems that dominoes have fallen by the wayside in the wake of video games and other fantasy-based competitions, they are very popular in Mexico. The same is true of *damas* (DAH-mahs), or checkers.

| | |
|---|---|
| **¡Bien hecho!** | Good play! |
| bee-EH NEH-cho | |
| **¡Juguemos de nuevo!** | Let's play again! |
| hoo-GHEH-mos deh NWEH-bo | |

**¡Vamos a jugar al póquer!** *(BAH-mo sah hoo-GAH rahl PO-kehr):* Let's play poker!

Turning our attention to cards, together with the "tame" games, the ones typically associated with gambling are quite popular, though Mexico doesn't have a Las Vegas to rival the one in the United States. But there are as many good players there as here, and it must be said that in a country where high-tech entertainments have only recently begun to distract even the well-to-do, there is potentially a higher percentage of the population that is still well versed in card games.

Drinking—heavy drinking—is not uncommon in such circumstances and among those who gamble, here or there. But serious gamblers seldom touch the stuff when they are at the tables, as any gambler reading this almost certainly knows. The names of most poker-like games are the same or are recognizable even in translation.

| | |
|---|---|
| **Prefiero veintiuno/blackjack.** | I prefer twenty-one/blackjack. |
| preh-fee-EH-ro BEYN-tee-OO-no/ blackjack | |
| **No me gusta apostar, gracias.** | I don't bet, thanks. |
| no meh GOOS-tah pos-TAHR GRAH-see-ahs | |

**¿Cuánto es la apuesta?** *(KWAHN-to ehs lah ah-PWEHS-tah):* What's the ante?

The more I learn about poker from reading about it and playing it, even among friends, the more convinced I am that I have no business playing it. However, there are professionals for whom the various forms of poker make it a game of skill, patience, and logical decision making more than a game of chance. I had a distant cousin who was a pro during the Depression. His motto was: "If you don't know everyone at the table, then *you're* the mark."

Gambling has its own culture, but its local or national variants. If you sit down to gamble with an amount you consider will amount to a serious *bote* (BO-teh), or pot, it is likely that it is an amount that is seen as even more serious to a gambler in Mexico. If you are a serious gambler, I highly recommend that you obtain a good list of the terms used in Mexico. There are several sites on the Internet that can help with that.

I have witnessed some interesting card games in Mexico, by which I mean that there are variants of card games that come from the Spanish and Italian traditions. They even have a different deck, made up of forty cards, not fifty-two. The Spanish deck is often a work of art, and some people, like me, collect them as objects of art. The moral of this story, which no gambler needs to hear, is don't risk money while learning a new game!

| | |
|---|---|
| **¡A barajar y cortar!** | Shuffle and cut! |
| ah bah-ra-HAH ree kor-TAHR | |
| **¿Quién es el dador?** | Who's the dealer? |
| kee-EH-neh sehl dah-DOR | |

**¡Vamos al hipódromo!** *(BAH-mo sah lee-PO-dro-mo)*: Let's go to the horse races!

The horse racing arena, for lack of a better translation of *hipódromo*, is not just about horse racing. It is a sort of community center at large, especially in northern Mexico. You could classify it as a stadium in which horses or cars can race, but where there are ample seating and facilities for a rock or country music concert.

Many national and international music artists give concerts in them. The websites of the *hipódromos* of Ciudad Juárez (across the Río Grande from El Paso) or the possibly most famous one in Hermosillo (in the state of Sonora, south of Arizona) can give you a clear idea of what sort of events they host and the types of crowds they draw.

160

It might or might not amuse some readers to learn that men pay more to enter than women, and kids get in free. If you don't enjoy horse racing, the *hipódromo* still may have cultural events with a lot of local color to make for a memorable and educational visit.

**¿Hay un concierto esta semana?**　Is there a concert this week?
ay yoon kon-see-EHR-to EHS-tah
　　seh-MAH-nah

**¿Tiene información sobre los**　Do you have information about the
　**caballos en inglés?**　　horses in English?
tee-EH-neh eem-for-mah-see-ON
　　SO-breh los kah-BAH-yo seh
　　neeng-GLEHS

**¿Dónde puedo apostar sobre**　Where can I bet on the race?
　**la carrera?**
DON-deh PWEH-thoh ah-pos-TAHR
　　SO-breh lah kah-RREH-rah

# Chapter 18

# Pyramids and Ruins

✈ **¿Hay un tour de Teotihuacán/Chichén Itzá en inglés?**
*(ay yoon toor theh teh-o-tee-hoo-wah-KAHN/chee-CHE neet-SAH ehn eeng-GLEHS):* Is there an English-language tour of Teotihuacán/Chichén Itzá?

Most tours have bilingual guides, so you're in for a treat if you go to any of the major sites. There are many tour packages available online that feature professional archaeologists as tour guides.

Compared with Egyptian archaeology, Mesoamerican archaeology is just coming of age. The decipherment of Mayan hieroglyphs was stalled for decades because of academic wrangling, to put it succinctly. Despite the destruction wrought by the Conquest, the Spanish also recorded a great deal of information that has aided scholars as starting points for their research in many cases. Despite the relative lack of information about the origins of many places, of which Teotihuacán is a prime example, more and more work is bringing to light new information and revising previously held notions about the Toltecs, Mayas, Aztecs, and other indigenous groups. The language of the Aztecs, Náhuatl (NAH-whah-tul), is still spoken.

163

Teotihuacán is the Náhuatl name for the complex of structures in the Anáhuac area, or the Mexican Basin (in and around Mexico City). The Aztecs did not build it—in fact, the whole area was already in ruins when they arrived. No one knows the name of the civilization that built these huge structures, rivals of Egypt's pyramids. On the other hand, it is known that Chichén Itzá, on the Yucután peninsula about 125 miles from Cancún and 75 miles from Mérida, was built by the Mayas.

**Hable más fuerte, por favor.**
Speak louder, please.
AH-bleh mahs FWEHR-teh por
   fah-BOR

 **¿Por qué practicaban el sacrificio humano?** *(por KEH prahk-tee-KAH-bah nehl sah-kree-FEE-see-o oo-MAH-no):* Why did they practice human sacrifice?

Yes, the Aztecs practiced human sacrifice. The "theological" justifications for it, from an anthropological or mythological perspective, are eclipsed by the fact that its use was an instrument of control and domination over the other groups this warrior tribe had conquered. The legendary story of Quetzalcóatl suggests a bringer of agriculture, civilization, law, technology, astronomy, and so forth.

There is some evidence to suggest that, just as in many other parts of the world, there were foundational and dedicatory sacrifices, evidenced by human remains found in or near the foundations of many structures. But the type of sacrifices one generally thinks of, with the gruesome removal of a beating heart, torn out by an obsidian knife studded with jade and turquoise, really did happen—and often.

**¿Tenían diosas los aztecas/mayas?**   Did the Aztecs/Mayas have
teh-NEE-ahn dee-O-sahs los                 goddesses?
   ahs-TEH-kahs/MAH-yas

**Muéstreme dónde está en el mapa.** *(MWEHS-treh-meh*
*THOHN-dehs-TAH eh nehl MAH-pah):* Show me where it is on
the map.

On the ground, things can look very different from what you imag-
ined when looking at a map. Unless you really think about the scale,
a place can seem much larger or smaller than expected. That isn't just
an academic problem when you want to walk around, enjoy yourself,
and still get back to the bus in time. Having a buddy system is a good
idea whether you're swimming or traveling.

**¿Cuánto se tarda caminando allá?**   How long does it take to get there
KWAHN-to seh TAHR-dah                      on foot?
   kah-mee-NAHN-do ah-YA

**¿Cuál es la pirámide del Sol/de la Luna?** *(KWAH lehs lah*
*pee-RAH-mee-deh dehl sol/deh la LOO-nah):* Which is the Pyramid of
the Sun/Moon?

As mentioned earlier, Mexico's pyramids are best represented by
those at the complex of Teotihuacán. This vast complex attracts many
people from around the world, particularly at the summer solstice,
but also at the winter one as well.

   The first main attraction there is the Avenue of the Dead, which
defines the complex by dividing it more or less symmetrically. The
regular design of the whole complex, even as it continues to be exca-

vated, suggests that it was fully designed from inception; in other words, it did not grow haphazardly like medieval European cities.

Once you are oriented to the cardinal points and to their relationship with the complex, the next attractions are the spectacular Pyramids of the Sun and the Moon, as well as the Pyramid of the Feathered Serpent, with its exquisite relief sculptures. Although the feathered serpent is best known to the modern world by its Aztec name Queztalcóatl (*quetzal* is the name of a very real tropical bird with bright green feathers; *coatl* is the generic Náhuatl word for snake), the serpent motif and its relationship to cosmology were common in earlier times. One suggestive cosmological connection is the northern circumpolar constellation we know as Draco.

**¿Para qué servían estas pirámides?**
What were these pyramids for?

PAH-rah KEH sehr-BEE-ah NEHS-tahs
pee-RAH-mee-dehs

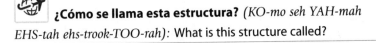 **¿Cómo se llama esta estructura?** *(KO-mo seh YAH-mah EHS-tah ehs-trook-TOO-rah):* What is this structure called?

While maps of the complexes in Mexico are plentiful, they don't necessarily show every structure. Many commercial tours will hit the highlights, of course. The ones led by professional archaeologists are predictably more detailed, but naturally they will leave some things out in the interest of time and relative importance.

Many maps and plans of the complexes are downloadable if you have time to do so in advance of a trip. I highly recommend doing as much reading as possible before you travel to see archaeological sites because if you don't, you'll feel like you're drinking from a fire hose—there is so much to learn!

The complex at Chichén Itzá is one of the seven wonders of the New World and contains three main attractions. The Castle, or *castillo* (kahs-TEE-yo), was dedicated to the Mayan god Kukulkán (the Aztecs would later call him Quetzalcóatl, or the Plumed Serpent). It was constructed so that following sunrise at the two equinoxes, a shadow forms as the sun strikes a wall and creeps up the steps, creating the image of an undulating serpent. If you go to Chichén Itzá, try to do so at that time. To ensure success at witnessing this phenomenon, go the day before and stay in one of the hotels in the area.

The Temple of Warriors is another structure, known for its square columns and relief sculptures of warriors bedecked in feathers. Finally, the famous Ball Court with its perfect acoustics is another major attraction. You can hear a whisper even at a distance of nearly 550 feet from one end to another. This is especially remarkable considering that it is not an elliptical or parabolic structure, but rectangular.

| | |
|---|---|
| **¿Fue un templo o un observatorio?** | Was it a temple or an observatory? |
| FWEH oon TEHM-plo o oo nob-sehr-bah-TO-ree-o | |

**¿Cómo funcionaba el sistema matemático?** *(KO-mo foon-see-o-NAH-bah ehl sees-TEH-mah mah-teh-MAH-tee-ko)*: How did their mathematical system work?

The Mayas had an ingenious number system; one reason they were capable astronomers was because they could do large calculations quickly. The system is simple in that it used only three symbols—

shells, dots and bars—but it was not based on ten. Perhaps your tour guide can show you actual examples of numbers in glyphs or in printed versions of astronomical charts.

The Mayas, and the Aztecs who succeeded them and adopted much of their culture, calculated the motions and phases of the moon, Venus, the constellations and, of course, the path of the Sun, the visible manifestation of Quetzalcóatl.

The Aztecs seemed to be obsessed with numbers and cyclical time in a way that spelled their doom: they were fatalistic. Cortés's arrival was seen as the return of the "undead" Quetzalcóatl who had, so to speak, picked up his bones and lived again.

**¿Cómo se representaban los números?**    How did they write their numbers?

KO-mo seh rreh-preh-sehn-TAH-bahn
   los NOO-meh-ros

**¿Por qué/Cómo/Cuándo desapareció esta civilización?**
(*por KEH/KO-mo/KWAHN-do deh-sah-pah-reh-see-O EHS-tah see-bee-lee-sah-see-ON*): Why/How/When did this civilization disappear?

As more sites are excavated and the work of deciphering many of the glyphs and codices advances, the answers to these questions are beginning to emerge. Estimates of population for the Teotihuacán complex suggest that it was one of the largest settled areas on Earth at its zenith. Likewise, the Mayan complexes, such as Chichén Itzá in the Yucatán or Tikal in Guatemala, had to have sizeable populations and diversified labor. The possible answers to the questions surrounding the demise of these places are numerous and intriguing.

If you have a professional guide, you will be treated to a vision into the past, almost as if into another planet. As you gather the pieces in your mind, try to imagine the surprise of the Spanish as they entered an empire larger than most nations of Europe!

**¿Es solamente una teoría o se**      Is it only a theory or has it been
   **ha probado?**      proven?

ehs so-lah-MEHN-teh oo-nah
   teh-o-REE-ah o seh ah
   pro-BAH-thoh

**¿Se puede/Se permite entrar/subir aquí?** *(seh PWEH-theh/seh pehr-MEE-teh ehn-TRAHR/soo-BEER ah-KEE):* Can one/Is one allowed to enter/climb here?

Restricted archaeological sites are usually roped off or otherwise marked better than some street repairs; such is Mexico's love for her past. There may be areas where freely wandering tourists ought not to venture, but this is usually not in the pyramid areas.

That said, if you have asthma or any medical condition that makes climbing steps difficult, be advised that the pyramids are steep and that even some students get winded climbing to their summits. Add to the steep climb the heat and the amount of walking one can do in some complexes, and you have a recipe for heatstroke or sunstroke. The best advice for people from northern climes is to slow down until you get used to the changes the heat will make in your metabolism, particularly in your intake of liquids.

**¿Se sigue excavando en este sitio?**  Is this site still being excavated?
seh SEE-gheh eks-kah-BAHN-do eh
   nehs-teh SEE-tee-o

**¿Cuánto mide esta pirámide/este templo?** *(KWAH-to MEE-theh EHS-tah pee-RAH-mee-deh/EHS-teh TEHM-plo):* How big is this pyramid/temple?

If you have looked online at statistical data about the complexes you are seeing, you probably will have fewer questions and you'll be going there mostly to take it all in for yourself. On the other hand, you might be a statistics junkie or an engineering-minded person. After all, getting into the details—the facts on the ground—about archaeological sites is one of the most important parts of archaeology.

Another branch of archaeology that is interdisciplinary, and therefore usually involves a team, is known as archaeoastronomy. It deals with man-made structures and their celestial alignments.

**Si no tenían la rueda, ¿cómo la construyeron?**
If they didn't have the wheel, how did they build it?

see no teh-NEE-ahn lah RRWEH-thah KO-mo lah kons-troo-YEH-ron

**¿Cuántas personas vivían en estos lugares?** *(KWAHN-tahs pehr-SO-nahs bee-BEE-ah neh NEHS-tos loo-GAH-rehs):* How many people lived in these places?

There are many estimates of the number of people living in what is now Mexico when Cortés landed in 1519. One estimate is fifteen million. The temple and observatory complexes, as well as the pyramids, have always posed a problem for archaeologists studying Mesoamerica because of a lack of evidence of housing. The conclusion has generally been that these places were sparsely populated except at important times. The counterargument is that it isn't logical to expend such vast resources on a place that stands relatively empty.

Then there is the great mystery surrounding their demise. It would be wonderful to know what all the tour guides say who might be asked these questions, even if the facts of archaeology aren't established by consensus.

**¿Eran ciudades o centros religiosos?**

Were they cities or religious centers?

EH-rahn see-oo-THA-deh so SEHN-tros rreh-lee-hee-O-sos

# Chapter 19

# Seaside: Diving, Sunbathing, and Surfing

**¿Cuál es la mejor playa para surfear/tomar el sol?**
*(KWAH lehs la meh-HOR PLAH-yah PAH-rah soor-feh-AHR/to-MAH rehl sol):* Which is the best beach for surfing/sunbathing?

Not all beaches are equally suitable for every type of beach or water-related sport. Whether for aesthetic reasons, safety, or just because what you want to do might be better done on this beach or that, it is good to ask a few questions. I grew up on Oahu—trust me.

Know what you're planning to do at the beach. Sunbathing? Then rocky beaches are not a good choice. Surfing? Find out about tides, rocks, reefs, currents, and so on.

**¿Cómo son las corrientes en esa playa?**
KO-mo son lahs ko-rree-EHN-teh seh NEH-sah PLAH-yah

What are the currents like at that beach?

| | |
|---|---|
| **¿Hay áreas restringidas/ prohibidas?** | Are there restricted/forbidden areas? |

ah YAH-reh-ahs rrehs-treeng-
HEE-thahs/pro-ee-BEE-thahs

**Necesito alquilar equipo para bucear.** *(neh-seh-SEE-to ahl-kee-LAH reh-KEE-po PAH-rah boo-seh-AHR):* I need to rent diving gear.

A quick visit to the Internet will show you how many diving tour companies there are just waiting to show you the undersea wonders lying off Mexican beaches. The continental shelf off the west coast of North America extends from Mexico to Canada, so most of what you will see, if you are a California diver, will be like California. If you have gone to Aruba or other terrific Caribbean diving spots, the gulf areas around Mexico will be similar.

If you go on an organized trip, your cares are probably few in terms of equipment. If you are an experienced diver but have not gone to Mexico, particularly the areas around Yucatán (Cozumel, in particular), then you are in for a treat. Most scuba shops will have English-speaking personnel is such places, but not everyone you walk up to will speak English.

Amateurs, newcomers, or hobbyists who like to snorkel, but not scuba, will also have a great time, provided they clearly understand where to go and not to go.

| | |
|---|---|
| **¿Manejan esnórqueles/máscaras?** | Do you carry snorkels/masks? |

mah-NEH-hah nehs-NOR-keh-lehs/
MAHS-kah-rahs

**¿Dónde puedo llenar estos tanques?**

DON-deh PWEH-thoh yeh-NAH rehs-tos TAHNG-kehs

Where can I fill these tanks?

**Se me rompió la aleta de mi tabla de surf.** *(seh meh rrom-pee-O lah ah-LEH-tah theh mee TAH-blah theh soorf):* I broke my surfboard fin.

It's a bummer if your board breaks while you're on vacation. If you're a really avid surfer, you probably have more than a couple of surfboards. Modern designs, including a number of different types of skegs, or surfboard fins, make riding different types of waves a bigger thrill than ever. Another word you might hear for surfboard fin, instead of *aleta,* is *orza* (OR-sah).

Like California, Mexico has some great surfing spots, particularly on the Pacific coast because of its gradually rising continental shelf. There are Mexican surfers, but when I surfed, they seemed far outnumbered by Californians. If you don't take an extra board, or a small repair kit for dings and an extra skeg, you might end up having to buy one south of the border.

**Necesito una nueva tabla de surf.**

neh-seh-SEE-to OO-nah NWEH-bah TAH-blah theh soorf

I need a new surfboard.

**¿Cuánto se tardará en hacer eso?**

KWAHN-to seh tahr-dah-RAH eh nah-SEHR EHS-o

How long will that take?

**¿Manejan bloques de cera?** *(mah-NEH-hahn BLO-kehs theh SEH-rah):* Do you carry surfboard wax?

A surf vacation is like no other. Remember the movie *Endless Summer*? On the road, though, you'll either realize you forgot something or you'll simply run out of supplies. The material that tether cords are made from, that bungee-type cord, is sometimes known as bungee, sometimes as tether—it all depends on how acquainted a surf shop clerk is with the lingo of English-speaking surfers. English leads the way in the surfing world, just as it dominated the Internet for a long time. One sign that a shop might know a great deal about supplies, suppliers, beaches, and so forth is whether or not they carry English-language magazines about the sport.

**¿Se vende óxido de cinc?**        Do you carry zinc oxide?
seh BEHN-deh OK-see-do theh seengk

 **Quiero aprender a surfear/bucear.** *(kee-EH-ro ah-prehn-DEH rah soor-feh-AHR/boo-seh-AHR):* I want to learn to surf/dive.

Newbies to surfing, windsurfing, diving, and even snorkeling need to have lessons. You don't learn all you need to know in an hour. Perhaps a snorkeling lesson of fifteen minutes will teach you all you need to know if you are going to be exploring shallow, well protected areas. But *perhaps* is the operative word. A lot of people forget the simple lesson that all cetaceans can teach us if only we are observant: blow out just before your snorkel tip reaches the surface.

If you need instruction, particularly in diving or surfing, it is good to find a bilingual instructor. Little details often don't communicate well just by imitating.

**¿Cuándo será disponible un instructor bilingüe?**

KWAHN-do seh-RAH dees-po-
NEE-bleh oon eens-trook-TOHR
bee-LEENG-gweh

When will a bilingual instructor be available?

**¿Cuánto tiempo dura una lección?**

KWAHN-to tee-EHM-po DOO-rah
OO-nah lehk-see-ON

How long is a lesson?

**Queremos navegar en barco de vela.** *(keh-REH-mos nah-beh-GAH rehn BAHR-ko theh BEH-lah):* We want to go sailing.

If you plan to sail, and are an experienced sailor, I have nothing to tell you about what to do on board. However, if you plan to hire a boat with a captain, then my advice is to brush up on your skills, or at least strengthen your resolve, for bargaining. If you have ever hired a deep-sea fishing boat from a U.S. port, you know there is a lot of competition among boat owners to get passengers and fishermen. Imagine that competition multiplied by a number of factors: you don't know the language and the vendors are usually more aggressive in Mexico, anxious to close a deal.

If you are a couple looking for a romantic cruise aboard a "brand name" ship, those are easier and less stressful to arrange, since the prices are fixed. Even if your decision to go is a last-minute one, something can usually be had from most major ports. Inquire of your hotel staff and they likely will point you to a variety of choices.

**¿Es posible alquilar un barco con capitán?**
Is it possible to hire a boat with a captain?

ehs po-SEE-bleh ahl-kee-LAH room BAHR-ko kon kah-pee-TAHN

**Quisiera una excursión de lujo muy romántica.**
I'd like to book a luxury romantic excursion.

kee-see-EH-rah OO-nah ehs-koor-see-ON deh LOO-ho moo-ee rro-MAHN-tee-kah

**Quiero comprarme un bañador/traje de baño.** *(kee-EH-ro kom-PRAHR-meh OON bahn-yah-THOR/TRAH-heh theh BAHN-yo):* I want to buy a bathing suit.

At the risk of sounding prudish—which I am not—before you buy a bathing suit in Mexico, take a look at what men and women are wearing at the beach or beaches you plan to go to. Remember, nude bathing is illegal. Don't try it. If you get caught, you will pay a fine and do a short jail term.

The bathing suit lesson is applicable to dress in Mexico in general: try to fit in. If you stand out, you attract attention and often that means the wrong sort. This is even more important for women. "Going native" does not mean buying traditional Mexican clothes or jewelry and wearing it. You'll be even more conspicuous. Just look around at how Mexicans dress at the beach or on the street and you'll get a quick idea.

Men, don't wear shorts or go barefoot anywhere but at the beach. Women, as a rule, bikinis are acceptable in areas with a heavy tourist population, but unlike in Waikiki, don't even think about walking across the street from the beach to your hotel, or going through your hotel lobby, in a bikini.

| | |
|---|---|
| **¿Manejan chancletas/huaraches?** | Do you carry sandals? |
| mah-NEH-hahn chang-KLEH-tahs/ | |
|    hoo-ah-RAH-chehs | |
| **Necesitamos toallas grandes** | We need beach towels for |
|    **para tomar el sol.** |    sunbathing. |
| neh-seh-see-TAH-mos to-AH-yahs | |
|    GRAHN-dehs PAH-rah to-MAH | |
|    rehl SOL | |

**¿Dónde se venden refrescos?** *(DON-deh seh BEHN-dehn rreh-FREHS-kos):* Where do they sell soft drinks?

Beachside vendors abound, it's true, but they don't all sell the same items. Many sell only one product: soft drinks at one stand, popsicles or grilled meats, and so on, at another.

One product I highly recommend, and that can be as delicious as a glass of fruit juice on a hot summer morning, or even better: *paletas* (pah-LEH-tahs). *Paletas* are Mexico's great improvement on the Popsicle. They are made from fresh fruit and they aren't just frozen juice, or worse, frozen juice concentrate. They are delicious, always locally made, and there are dozens of flavors. Usually there are several places that make them in town and you can see them being made, a double treat for kids, like a field trip to the ice-cream factory. Better yet, they are cheap!

**Me gustaría una paleta de mango.**     I'd like a mango Popsicle.

meh goos-tah-REE-ah OO-nah

    pah-LEH-tah theh MAHN-go

**Deme agua mineral.**               Give me mineral water.

DEH-meh AH-gwah mee-neh-RAHL

**¿Dónde se venden/alquilan parasoles para la playa?**

*(DON-deh seh BEHN-dehn/ahl-KEE-lahn pah-rah-SO-lehs PAH-rah lah PLAH-yah):* Where do they sell/rent beach umbrellas?

Sometimes, in the interest of packing light, you can plan on buying or renting a lot of the things you might need on vacation. Aside from buying travel sizes of toiletries, it might be a comfort to know that you can buy lotion and other beach necessities at any resort city or town. Unless you need a particular brand of cosmetics, relax; Mexico is a land of sun and tourism is big business. They haven't forgotten that you probably need to either protect yourself from UV rays or harness them by applying sunscreen or suntan oil.

    Besides the hotel or a local pharmacy, there are often beachside rental stands that supply many of the basics. You really don't want to take a beach umbrella on the plane, do you?

**¿Hay una buena loción**        Is there a good tanning lotion?
    **bronceadora?**

ay YOO-nah BWEH-nah lo-see-ON

    bron-seh-ah-THO-rah

**No quiero broncearme.**        I do not want to tan.

no kee-EH-ro bron-seh-AHR-meh

**¿Adónde voy para practicar el paracaidismo acuático?**

*(ah-THON-deh boy PAH-rah prahk-tee-KAH rehl pah-rah-kah-ee-DEES-mo ah-KWAH-tee-ko):* Where can I go parasailing?

Extreme sports are not the invention of crazy gen-X *gringos*. Remember the cliff divers of Acapulco? They're still there. Anyway, there are a few somewhat less extreme sports than that, or bungee jumping. Aquaplaning, hang gliding, and parasailing are all very popular in most seaside resorts. If you plan to jet ski, be sure to find out the restricted areas, since they are often kept clear of swimmers, surfers, and skiers.

It was once politely "recommended" to me that I leave a surfing area in Mexico, not for using a motorized vehicle, but for bodysurfing in the midst of surfers, something I did all the time growing up in Hawaii. Come to think of it, bodysurfing among boards wasn't the best idea then either, as one skeg scar on my back still reminds me.

**Me gustaría ir en acuaplano.**
meh goos-tah-REE-ah ee reh
    nah-kwah-PLAH-no

I'd like to go on the hydroplane.

**¿Cuánto cuesta alquilar los
    jet esquí?**
KWAHN-to KWEHS-tahl kee-LAHR
    los YEH-tehs-kee

How much does it cost to rent the
    jet skis?

# Chapter 20

# Conversational Phrases

**¡Qué interesante!** *(keh een-teh-reh-SAHN-teh):* How interesting!

If you're trying to speak a little Spanish, and for you a phrasebook is something like having a pair of training wheels, you might be very successful in the art of conversation. You'll have more success if the person with whom you happen to chat is about as good at English as you are at Spanish because you'll spend some time negotiating meaning.

One definition of the art of conversation is how to not necessarily say anything at all. That's obviously an exaggeration, but the grain of truth that may be lurking in that observation is that good conversationalists learn to ask questions more than talk themselves. Phrases that elicit more speech from your conversational partner are the ones that generally make them feel that you are a good listener and that you are interested in what they have to say.

**Me fascina esto.**                    This is fascinating.

meh fahs-SEE-nah EHS-to

**Me choca esto.**
meh CHO-kah EHS-to

This bothers me a lot.

**¡Fantástico!/¡Magnífico!**
fahn-TAHS-tee-ko/mahg-NEE-fee-ko

Fantastic!/Magnificent!

**¡Qué aburrido!**
keh ah-boo-REE-thoh

How boring!

**¡No me diga!** *(no meh DEE-gah)*: You don't say!

Conversational Spanish goes beyond any phrasebook, of course, so it is only likely to happen when you're at the beach, for instance, or on a plane or in a bar, essentially whenever and wherever you have no pressing business, linguistically speaking, and therefore have the luxury of some time to try to talk and a sympathetic conversation partner.

If you want to go beyond a curt *yes* and *no* in conversational Spanish, use *Simón* for *yes* and *nopales* for *no*. *Simón* is simply a play on the proper name, and *nopales* is the name of the cactus on Mexico's national seal. It may seem a little corny until you recall such English expressions as *yep* and *nope*. For a little fun, the last phrase I've included in the group below literally means "pure potatoes."

**Es la pura verdad.**
ehs lah POO-rah behr-THAHD

It's the gospel truth.

**Así es.**
ah-SEE ehs

That's how it is.

**¿No es cierto?**
no ehs see-EHR-to

Isn't that right?

**Son puras papas.**
son POO-rahs PAH-pahs

Pure nonsense!

**¿En serio?** *(ehn SEH-ree-o):* Seriously?

Besides being able to elicit more information, you need confirmation and transitional phrases to change the subject or take your turn. Idiomatic or slang expressions abound in casual conversation. There are thousands—if not tens of thousands—of such expressions in most languages. Many of them are colorful, particularly when contrasted with their English counterparts. If you add to idiomatic or slang expressions all the possibilities and potential that exists in proverbs, literary allusions, or historical or pop-culture references, it is easy to see how a person can feel that a year in a foreign language class didn't begin to scratch the surface when it comes to becoming fluent in a foreign language.

But take heart! If you studied Spanish in high school or college in a decent program and paid attention, then you did lay a solid foundation for communicating. The last one in the following list is a fun one when you compare it to its English counterpart. The Spanish literally means "You're taking me by the hair."

| | |
|---|---|
| **¿De veras?** | Really? |
| deh BEH-rahs | |
| **De hecho...** | In fact . . . |
| deh EH-cho | |
| **A propósito...** | By the way . . . |
| ah pro-PO-see-to | |
| **Me está tomando el pelo.** | You're pulling my leg. |
| mehs-TAH to-MAHN-do ehl PEH-lo | |

**Tiene/No tiene razón.** *(tee-EH-neh/no tee-EH-neh rrah-SON):* You are/aren't right.

A good conversationalist doesn't have to agree all the time; just be agreeable as a conversational partner. How to disagree without being disagreeable goes way beyond any phrasebook, but at least you can have the linguistic tools to express your difference of opinion. Probably the best way to avoid being disagreeable is to not let it show at an emotional level.

The last phrase deserves special attention. It is most definitely a negative, unlike its English sound-alike *absolutely,* which always conveys strong agreement.

| | |
|---|---|
| **No lo creo./Lo dudo.** | I don't think so./I doubt it. |
| no lo KREH-o/lo THOO-thoh | |
| **¡Claro que sí/no!** | Certainly!/Certainly not! |
| CLAH-ro keh SEE/NO | |
| **¡En absoluto!** | Absolutely not! |
| eh nahb-so-LOO-to | |

**Me parece muy bien.** *(meh pah-REH-seh MOO-ee bee-EHN):* It seems fine to me.

Establishing your ground, clarifying where you stand, and showing that you understand the other person, or coming to an understanding of where each person stands on a subject, is a good way to lay the groundwork for a good conversation. It could even lead to a friendship.

In various sections of this phrasebook I have stressed that Mexicans tend to avoid personal conflict. This applies mainly to the finger-pointing type of conflicts where a person is singled out for blame. Mexicans are as fond as most people of lively exchange and, compared with many people in the United States, are quite willing to engage in political conversations.

One feature of Spanish is the use of certain words to indicate negatives and positives. The last phrase below shows how to express whether or not you also think or feel as the other person. The words *también* and *tampoco* are, with respect to their meaning, heads and tails of each other, but they are not interchangeable.

| | |
|---|---|
| **Creo que sí/no.** | I think so./I don't think so. |
| KREH-o keh SEE/NO | |
| **Estoy/No estoy de acuerdo.** | I agree./I don't agree. |
| ehs-TOY/no ehs-TOY theh | |
| ah-KWEHR-do | |
| **¿De acuerdo?** | Are we agreed?/Do you agree? |
| deh ah-KWEHR-do | |
| **Yo también./Yo tampoco.** | Me too./Me neither. |
| YO tahm-bee-EHN/YO tahm-PO-ko | |

**¡Parece mentira!** *(pah-REH-seh mehn-TEE-rah):* Seems impossible!

If something seems far-fetched, a "stretcher" as Mark Twain called it, it is best to let it pass. If your conversation partner is clearly somewhat incredulous of what he or she is relating, then it is probably safe to utter this expression. However, never omit the first word, *parece*, or it becomes an accusation of lying. The word *mentira* means *lie*.

Once upon a time, say, only a few generations ago, to say that word all by itself used to cause sword fights and duels. Today, it can still lead to nasty situations. To say *parece mentira* then, especially with some joviality in the voice, is to acknowledge the other person's incredulity or the oddness of what he or she is telling you and not to cast doubt on him or her.

| | |
|---|---|
| **¡Esto no puede ser!** | It can't be so!/No way! |
| EHS-to no PWEH-theh SEHR | |
| **Me lo dice en broma, ¿no?** | You're just kidding, right? |
| meh lo THEE-sehn BRO-mah no | |

**¿Y entonces?** *(ee yehn-TON-sehs):* And so/next/then?

It's good to have a short list of transitional phrases that don't commit you to any particular opinion, or that simply keep the other person talking while you think. Most people enjoy talking and telling stories, particularly about themselves, so if your aim is to engage a Mexican in conversation, it is to your advantage to let him or her do most of the talking, since you're the one at a linguistic disadvantage! Many people who travel abroad come back with a different perspective about what it means to be a foreigner as a result of their successes and failures when attempting to communicate.

| | |
|---|---|
| **¿Qué cree usted de esto?** | What do you think about this? |
| keh KREH oos-TEHD THEHS-to | |
| **¿Qué le parece a usted?** | How does it seem to you? |
| keh leh pah-REH-seh ah oos-TEHD | |
| **¿Qué opina usted de esto?** | What's your opinion of this? |
| keh o-PEE-nah oos-TEHD THEHS-to | |
| **¿No es mejor/peor así?** | Isn't it better/worse this way? |
| no ehs meh-HOR/peh-O rah-SEE | |

**Cuéntemelo todo.** *(KWEHN-teh-meh-lo TO-tho):* Do tell all.

If you have what you think is the beginning of a friendship, you may soon discover that Mexicans are somewhat more open than most Anglos about their fondness of rumors and gossip, or *chismes* (CHEES-mehs). Personally, I think Hispanics are just more honest about the fact that unwritten or unacknowledged truths and deeds are at least as powerful or important socio-politically as the headlines, and often more so. To be informed is to be forewarned, so paradoxically, they tend to be open about gossip.

**Lo quiero saber todo.**                I want to know everything./Tell all.
lo kee-EH-ro sah-BEHR TO-tho
**No entiendo.**                           I don't understand.
no ehn-tee-EHN-do
**¡A ver, a ver!**                          Let's see—out with it!
ah BEHR ah BEHR

 **Creo que se equivoca.** *(KREH-o keh seh kee-BO-kah):* I think you're mistaken.

If you have established enough goodwill that you can afford to disagree or call someone's exaggeration, or to express admiration for their knowledge, you can be ready with a few phrases like the ones in this section. It might be a good idea to admire the person's knowledge and wide reading before you express an objection.

Again, remember that Mexicans, just as people in almost all cultures, can disagree when face to face. At the same time, they make every effort to avoid making a disagreement appear to be a personal issue, because that would seem discourteous. A difference of opinion must always be made to appear as innocent as a difference in taste in food.

As we all know, Mexican politics is volatile. Just take a look at the local tabloids to get an idea of how personal and violent local politics can be. In those realms, things change quickly and become deeply personal, class conscious, and regional. But you're on vacation!

| | |
|---|---|
| **¿Dónde oyó usted esto?** | Where did you hear this? |
| DON-deh o-YO oos-TEHD EHS-to | |
| **Dudo que sea así.** | I doubt it's that way. |
| DOO-tho keh SEH-ah ah-SEE | |
| **Usted me parece bien informado.** | You sound like you know what |
| oos-TEHD meh pah-REH-seh | you're talking about. |
| bee-EH neem-for-MAH-tho | |
| **¡Usted exagera!** | You're exaggerating! |
| oos-TEHD ek-sah-HEH-rah | |

**¡Qué gracioso!** *(keh grah-see-O-so):* How funny/comical!

Finally, you should know and keep in mind that Mexicans have a great sense of humor. There is no political correctness in Mexico, but you will find no mean-spiritedness in their humor, regardless of how frank it is about the human condition. It is an acknowledged fact among theorists of comedy that someone has to be the butt of the joke, and upon hearing a joke of any kind in which someone inevitably suffers, you'll frequently hear a Mexican compassionately mutter while laughing heartily *¡Ay, pobre Diablo!* (AY PO-breh dee-AH-blo) (Oh, the Poor devil!)

**Es/No es muy chistoso eso.**     That is/isn't funny.

ehs/no ehs MOO-ee chees-TO-so
   EH-so

**No me llama la atención.**     It doesn't grab me.

no meh YAH-mah lah
   ah-tehn-see-ON

# The Right Phrase for
# Every Situation...Every Time.

Perfect Phrases for Building Strong Teams
Perfect Phrases for Business Letters
Perfect Phrases for Business Proposals and Business Plans
Perfect Phrases for Business School Acceptance
Perfect Phrases for College Application Essays
Perfect Phrases for Cover Letters
Perfect Phrases for Customer Service
Perfect Phrases for Dealing with Difficult People
Perfect Phrases for Dealing with Difficult Situations at Work
Perfect Phrases for Documenting Employee Performance Problems
Perfect Phrases for Executive Presentations
Perfect Phrases for Landlords and Property Managers
Perfect Phrases for Law School Acceptance
Perfect Phrases for Lead Generation
Perfect Phrases for Managers and Supervisors
Perfect Phrases for Managing Your Small Business
Perfect Phrases for Medical School Acceptance
Perfect Phrases for Meetings
Perfect Phrases for Motivating and Rewarding Employees
Perfect Phrases for Negotiating Salary & Job Offers
Perfect Phrases for Perfect Hiring
Perfect Phrases for the Perfect Interview
Perfect Phrases for Performance Reviews
Perfect Phrases for Real Estate Agents & Brokers
Perfect Phrases for Resumes
Perfect Phrases for Sales and Marketing Copy
Perfect Phrases for the Sales Call
Perfect Phrases for Setting Performance Goals
Perfect Phrases for Small Business Owners
Perfect Phrases for the TOEFL Speaking and Writing Sections
Perfect Phrases for Writing Grant Proposals
Perfect Phrases in American Sign Language for Beginners
Perfect Phrases in French for Confident Travel
Perfect Phrases in German for Confident Travel
Perfect Phrases in Italian for Confident Travel
Perfect Phrases in Spanish for Confident Travel to Mexico
Perfect Phrases in Spanish for Construction
Perfect Phrases in Spanish for Gardening and Landscaping
Perfect Phrases in Spanish for Household Maintenance and Childcare
Perfect Phrases in Spanish for Restaurant and Hotel Industries

**Visit mhprofessional.com/perfectphrases for a complete product listing.**

Learn more. Mc Graw Hill Do more.